2

EFFECTIVE PARENTS/ RESPONSIBLE CHILDREN

A Guide to Confident Parenting

ROBERT EIMERS
ROBERT AITCHISON, PH.D.

McGraw-Hill Book Company
NEW YORK/ST. LOUIS/SAN FRANCISCO
DÜSSELDORF/LONDON/MEXICO/
SYDNEY/TORONTO

Book design by Ingrid Beckman.

2 3 4 5 6 7 8 9 B P B P 7 8 3 2 1 0 9 8

First McGraw-Hill Paperback edition, 1978.

Library of Congress Cataloging in Publication Data

Eimers, Robert.
Effective parents/responsible children.

Includes index.
1. Discipline of children.   I. Aitchison, Robert,
joint author.   II. Title.
HQ770.4.E45   649'.1   76–44340
ISBN 0–07–019108–5

To our parents

LOIS MARIE AND ROBERT C. EIMERS
HILA BETH AND ROBERT C. AITCHISON

ACKNOWLEDGMENTS

THE AUTHORS WISH to acknowledge the kind support and advice of Dr. Robert Liberman, M.D. We also wish to thank Lou Ashworth for her suggestions and careful editing of the manuscript.

The authors have received support from grant number MH 26207–01 from the Mental Health Services Research and Development Branch of the National Institute of Mental Health and from a California Department of Health 314(d) grant. The opinions expressed in this book are those of the authors and do not reflect the official policy of the Regents of the University of California or the California Department of Health.

CONTENTS

SECTION 1
The Basic Skills

1 ◆§ §◆

An Overview

THIS BOOK IS for parents who genuinely love their children. It is for responsible parents who wish for nothing less than the healthiest and happiest of family relationships possible. Unfortunately, however, wishing alone doesn't always make it so. It has been our experience that, no matter how badly well-intentioned parents may want these things, all too often they encounter difficulties in achieving them. Let's face it: relationship-building is not easy. It requires a good deal of skill, patience, and, most important, an overriding concern for the growth and welfare of the child.

The basic premise of this book is that healthy and constructive parent-child interactions lead to warm and loving relationships. This in turn promotes the development of happier, more confident, and more secure children. In short, mutually rewarding family relationships are not just accidents. They are the *result* of positive interactions between parents and their children. However, the reverse is also true. Repeated parent-child interactions filled with scolding, tension, accusations, and unpredictable emotional outbursts can strain even the best of relationships. We all know that most parents don't want to seem cruel or inhuman, and it is for this reason that this book has been written.

Take a moment or two here to think about how much your children mean to you and how good they can make you feel. They make you laugh; they make you proud; they even make you presents. Your children care what you think, what you say, what you do, and how you are feeling. They love you, trust you, and miss you when you are gone. They probably come to you for just about everything from right answers and toy repairs to sympathy and first-aid. You've got to admit it; it's gratifying to be loved and needed like that. It's great to be a parent.

On the other hand, however, let's remember that family life is not always a bed of roses. Children are simply human and, of course, so are parents. And, as we all know, human beings have been known to get in each other's way or on each other's nerves at times. Of course, this happens in some families more than others, but we haven't heard of any families living in a totally hassle-free environment. What we are driving at here is simply this: Problems will and do arise; this you can count on. Furthermore, in the area of child misbehavior, these problems can create resentment, anger, and exhaustion in even the most patient of parents. To emphasize our point, we have assembled a short list of common, everyday occurrences which, if dealt with ineffectively, can lead to conflict, misunderstanding, and worst of all, negative feelings between parent and child. See if any of these situations sound familiar to you.

1. Your house is an absolute mess, and you are expecting company in about ten minutes. You have asked your two children to help you out by putting away their toys. The youngest jumps up and eagerly lends a hand, but the oldest ignores your request and continues to play with his toys. How would you handle this?

2. Just two days ago your daughter adopted the strategy of screaming, kicking, and throwing things whenever she couldn't have her way. You are beginning to grow weary of these tantrums, but there is no relief in sight.

3. Number One son has been pounding lumps on younger brother every day for quite some time now. You wish he'd find something else to occupy his time, but nothing you do or say to him seems to make any difference.

4. Your three-year-old has grown accustomed to a nightly regimen of bedtime stories, kisses, and multiple glasses of water. The entire ritual can often consume the better part of an hour. When you decide to cut this ceremony a little short, however, he insists on crying loudly and calling for you, until you finally are forced to give in just to shut him up.

5. Until recently, you have really enjoyed grocery shopping with your children. Lately, however, they have been swarming and whining like a squadron of mosquitoes. You hate to hire a baby-sitter just so you can shop, but what else can you do?

6. Your youngster has recently developed a rather effective tactic to avoid doing chores. Whether you ask him to take out the trash or cut the grass, he

invariably promises to do it later. Of course, he usually "forgets" to live up to his promises. Sound familiar?

7. Lately, whenever you are forced to turn down a request from your eleven-year-old daughter, she cries "I hate you," storms off to her room, and slams the bedroom door in the process. Whew!

As you probably well know, this list of problem situations is by no means exhaustive, yet the available research data suggest that this is a representative sampling. The point of this list is to start you thinking about what in particular your child does that is annoying to you, as well as point out that "problem" situations such as these are not unique to your family, but usually crop up at one time or another in almost every home. "All right," you may be saying to yourself, "that makes me feel a little better, but just because other parents are in the same boat doesn't mean that I'm not going to get annoyed or upset when Junior is being obnoxious, does it?" Well, to some extent that is true. It is only human for parents to be upset, aggravated, or even despondent when their children misbehave. Just as most parents have at least some difficulties with their children, research data also show that most parents have also experienced negative thoughts or feelings about their kids at one time or another. Have you ever caught yourself, for example, really disliking your child, and then felt guilty about it? Have you ever wished he would vanish into thin air? Do you find yourself saying "He'll outgrow it," when you know darn well you can't wait that long? Worse yet, have you ever wondered if it's all your fault, if you are simply a bad parent, and if now only a shrink can repair the damage you have done?

In short, it's O.K. to be upset with your children now and then. It is not O.K., however, to be upset with them constantly. Loving and concerned parents cannot afford to simply continue getting angry over repeated behavior problems. Instead, they can show their commitment and love by learning new and constructive ways to solve their interpersonal problems. At any rate, we simply want to reinforce the notion (1) that all available evidence indicates that it is not unusual for parents to encounter difficulties with their children at one time or another, and (2) that such parents are not inhuman, un-American, or antisocial if they happen to get upset about it. Effective parenting, however, is the best way we know to minimize the frequency and intensity of such occurrences.

The Rights of Children and Parents

Children need space and freedom to grow. They need an atmosphere of warmth and trust in which to freely express their thoughts and emotions. These same things, however, can also be said for parents. They, too, need space and freedom to grow. They, too, need a family climate conducive to the free expression of ideas and feelings. All too often, however, it seems the needs of parents are being sacrificed to the wishes and behavior of their children, or vice versa. Either way, the consequences are usually disastrous for both parent *and* child. Resentments build, tempers flare, and, in the final analysis, neither party gets what he or she really wants—a healthy and happy relationship with the other. In short, nobody wins. The point of all this is that a satisfactory balance must be obtained. For example, your decision to have children brought with it a number of responsibilities and commitments. Yet no one would argue that with that decision you were obligated to sell your personal happiness down the river. Each set of parents, then, must work this out for themselves, carefully balancing the needs of the child for optimal growth and development with their own needs for self-expression, harmony, and peace of mind.

With that thought in mind, a number of individuals from a broad range of disciplines have bombarded parents with all sorts of remedies and advice. Most of the early approaches to child-raising seemed to be based on various cardinal rules, platitudes, or moral guidelines. Remember when "spare the rod and spoil the child" was the only respected doctrine? Life seemed a lot simpler then. It was not long, however, before a host of self-appointed "experts" began warning parents of the irreparable harm they could inflict on their child's personality if they did not "spare the rod." Instead, it became fashionable to encourage parents to achieve insight into the underlying causes of Johnny's behavior. But did it really help the parents of an eight-year-old, for example, to realize that he was acting up simply because he had been denied his mother's breast and sentenced to endure the hardships of bottle-feeding before he was ready? Did that new understanding alter the present behavior patterns of the child or his parents in any way? Maybe—but, then again, maybe not. You can bet, however, that the parents felt a little more guilty. Essentially, what this approach had to offer was a highly sophisticated theory to explain the intricacies of the parent-child relationship.

But what about changing the relationship? In our quest for understanding did we come to forget about behavior change? Well, it seems that we did, at least for a while, but, as the amount of research in child psychology grew in size and sophistication, a powerful technology for behavior change began to emerge. Based on experimentally derived laws of learning, this technology soon made its way to the forefront of the field. The behavior-change approaches succeeded where others had failed for two very simple reasons: They were based on findings of scientific research, and they made specific recommendations about what parents could *do* to change their children's behavior. The number of behavior-change techniques has grown by leaps and bounds over the course of the past twenty years, yet the basic theoretical assumption has remained essentially the same, i.e., that a person's behavior is shaped by its consequences. One problem, though, is that simpler theories of rewards and punishments tend to lose out in raw interest value when they are compared to theories which talk about intrapsychic struggles, featuring primitive sex drives locked in eternal combat with a tyrannical superego. Now that's excitement! Or almost as intriguing are those approaches which teach you how to "relate" to your child like a shrink. Your youngster may be covering your living-room walls with graffiti, but that's O.K.; he's only "expressing himself," right? Only a meanie would stifle his budding creativity by punishing him. All kidding aside, there seem to be so many different "expert" approaches to child-raising that a bewildered parent looking for "the answer" in these times is not unlike a beggar in a cafeteria. He knows for sure that he's hungry, but he's having a hard time deciding what to eat.

"All right, all right," you may say to yourself. "That's nice to know. But exactly what does your book have to offer me that's so different?" Well, we are offering you a set of specific yet flexible parenting skills of proven effectiveness. These procedures are specific in the sense that parents are coached in *exactly* how to use them for optimal results. The skills are also flexible, however, so they can be employed in any number of everyday situations typically encountered by parents.

Perhaps an example from our own case files will show you what we mean, and how a parent can be confused by the wide range of approaches available. Mr. and Mrs. L. came to the clinic one day with a problem. For the past several years their son Tommy had developed the very annoying habit of never complying with their requests. At first, they had simply waited patiently for him to outgrow it, but this approach did not pay off. It seemed to them that nothing short of spanking the hell out of Tommy seemed to work. After months of experimenting on their own with a potpourri of strategies and techniques, Mr. and Mrs. L. finally admitted to themselves that Tommy's behavior had them over a barrel. At the urging of their pediatrician, they made an appointment for Tommy with a local child psychiatrist. To make a long story short, after months of play therapy at $35 an hour, the psychiatrist terminated his sessions with Tommy and instructed Mr. and Mrs. L. that Tommy was suffering from inadequate superego development caused by incomplete resolution of his Oedipal conflicts. Consequently, he went on, Mr. and Mrs. L. should "structure" Tommy as much as possible through limit-setting, while at the same time work on enhancing his self-concept by providing him with a number of "success experiences." Such an approach, they were told, would cause Tommy to feel more secure as well as give him the chance to grow and express himself. Well, needless to say the L.s were a little bit awed, as well as confused, by all this. After all, hadn't they been trying for months to set limits for him? And they'd love nothing more than to give him a few success experiences, but how? At any rate, they tried their best, but nothing seemed to change.

Then one day a compassionate neighbor told Mrs. L. about the parent training groups being conducted evenings at the local community mental health center. Although Mr. and Mrs. L. were somewhat skeptical of such approaches, the parent training course was free, and when they really thought about it, they realized they had nothing to lose. Again, to make a long story even shorter, Mr. and Mrs. L. were instructed in the ins and outs of rewards and punishments and then given a home program to change Tommy's behavior. And it worked! At first, it was heavenly; Mr. and Mrs. L. felt like they had gained a new lease on life. Several months later, however, the home program began to lose its appeal, as well as its effectiveness. Tommy had begun to agitate for bigger and better rewards for his compliance, and it was getting darn expensive. Mr. and Mrs. L. knew that they couldn't go on forever giving him candy, money, and/or privileges every time he did something right. For some reason, that idea just did not sit right with them. Of course, it had been explained to them in the parent group that they weren't really bribing Tommy to be good, but somehow they remained unconvinced. It looked like a bribe; it smelled like a bribe; it tasted like a bribe; it must *be* a bribe.

"What about the human touch?" they wondered. "What about relating to Tommy socially?" They decided to give it another try, and made an appointment to see us the following week. We listened empathically to Mr. and Mrs. L. as they recounted for us the train of events which finally brought them to us. Then we began a program designed to train Mr. and Mrs. L. in the proper use of some socially oriented parenting skills which are easy to learn, fun to practice, and, perhaps most important, proven powerful techniques for effecting behavior change, especially in children. The behavioral parent group had already given Mr. and Mrs. L. a thorough grounding in the principles of changing behavior, and they had been taught to implement these principles via tangible rewards such as money, toys, etc. Building on this foundation, we simply added the much-needed human touch. By gradually phasing out the program of candy and cash prizes and replacing it with a set of flexible parenting skills, the saga of Mr. and Mrs. L. soon came to a happy ending. Tommy's behavior improved, but the icing on the cake was that Mr. and Mrs. L. also reported feeling much closer to their child. In short, they all like each other better. Tommy, in particular, has benefited from these changes. He's now a happy and secure child.

The point of this example, which also happens to be the rationale for this book, is that, for most parents, being told why your child behaves the way he does, or even being told what to do about it, is often not enough. Parents want and need to know the *how*, exactly how, to deal with their children. Tommy's psychiatrist, for example, knew what he was talking about. Tommy really did need limit-setting and success experiences, but Mr. and Mrs. L. needed to know more specifics, mainly *how to do it*. The parent training group was also valuable, teaching them the fundamental principles and techniques of behavior change. The home program developed at the group was really quite useful in setting limits and providing success experiences. Yet its emphasis on tangible rewards coupled with its relative neglect of social interaction made Mr. and Mrs. L. uneasy, as well as making Tommy a little greedy. What Mr. and Mrs. L. really needed was some systematic coaching on how to respond more appropriately to Tommy's behavior. By actively practicing with us such details as what they might say, where to stand in relation to the child, how to incorporate nonverbal gestures into their communication, appropriate facial expressions, and so on, Mr. and Mrs. L. had soon mastered parenting skills which are flexible enough to accommodate a wide variety of situations and settings. Furthermore, since they had been coached in the specific details of using these procedures, they were now knowledgeable enough to offer constructive and helpful comments to each other right on the spot.

Because of our success with a number of concerned parents like Mr. and Mrs. L., we have put together for you a complete set of parenting procedures which are both simple and effective. These parenting skills will be explicitly described for you in subsequent pages, including such details as what you should say and when you've said too much. We have also developed and refined a training procedure which, if closely followed, will permit you to practice and master these important techniques.

We are confident about the effectiveness of the procedures outlined in this book. They work, and the evidence from psychological research supports this contention. Nevertheless, one must bear in mind that there exists no single system of solutions to all problems involving children. Human relationships are simply too complex for that. We have found, however, that, by practicing certain concrete steps of parenting, parents are more prepared to deal with the multitude of decisions and problems that make up every parent's waking day. In short, what we are offering here is a set of useful skills which, if employed in a patient and loving context, can do much to prevent family discord and establish more harmonious parent-child relationships.

This book has been designed on a do-it-yourself format. Each chapter will contain a number of exercises for you to do. *Please do the exercises.* Our research shows that parents who actually *practice* our parenting skills learn them far better than those who simply read about them. We expect no less of you, our readers, than we expect of our clinic clients. You have an advantage, however, in that you can practice and refine your parenting skills in the privacy of your own home. With that thought in mind, let's move on to Chapter Two.

2 ᭥᭥

---

*Why Do Kids Do
What They Do?*

OUR PARENTING TECHNIQUES have been derived from the laws of human behavior. A firm grasp of a few fundamental principles will add not only to a better understanding of your child's behavior, but also to the ease with which you develop and refine the important parenting skills presented in this book. With that thought in mind, let us take a few moments here to outline some of the reasons why children do the things that they do.

The Truth about Consequences

Behavior is shaped by its consequences. This simple, commonsense statement tells you just about all you need to know about human behavior. What does it mean? Simply this: If you do something, be it going to a party, kissing your spouse, or even scratching your nose, whatever happens to you as a consequence (or result) of that behavior will determine how likely you will be to behave that way again in the future. There's a great deal of scientific research backing up this statement, and understanding it is the key to understanding human behavior. Behavior is shaped by its consequences. Remember that; it's important.

The Concept of Rewards

Knowing that behavior is shaped by its consequences, we can now go one step further. If you behave a certain way and something *good* happens to you as a result, you will be more likely to do that same thing again. A trained porpoise, for example, knows that if he jumps through a hoop, his trainer will reward him with a fish dinner. Sure, you probably wouldn't jump through any hoops for just a mouthful of raw fish, but take a minute or two here to think about all the things you do in your daily life, and then see if you can figure out the various rewards you get which make doing those things worthwhile. We go to work, for example, because we get paid for that behavior. We ask a question, and the answer is our reward. We say nice things to people so they'll like us. The list is virtually endless. Let's take a closer look, however, at an example of how a child's behavior is affected by rewards.

Michael is an eager-to-please four-year-old who has spent his entire afternoon working on a finger-painting to give to his dad when he comes home from work. When Dad rewards Michael's efforts with a big smile, a hug, or lots of praise, chances are that Michael not only feels pretty good about himself, but he's already looking forward to making his dad more nice presents in the future.

How long do you think Michael would continue to do nice things like this for his dad if all he got was a perfunctory "Oh, that's nice" as his reward? Probably not too long. Once the rewards which serve to maintain a behavior stop coming in, that behavior is not likely to occur again. In short, if you want to see more of a particular behavior from someone, make sure that he feels he's been amply rewarded for that behavior.

When a Reward Is Not a Reward

One word of caution is in order before we leave the topic of rewards. One man's meat may well be another man's poison. Let's take the case of the well-meaning but unliberated husband as an example. Lately, it seems that his wife has been getting up early on weekends to cook him up a scrumptious breakfast, and boy, does he like that behavior! Knowing full well that this behavior is more likely to continue if it's rewarded, hubby figures that he'd better get on the stick and do something nice for his wife in return. So he decides to take her out to a hockey game. Big reward—she hates hockey. A big hug and a kiss after breakfast not only would have been a bit more appropriate, but also would have gone a lot further toward inspiring his wife to keep on cooking those great breakfasts for him.

The Concept of Punishment

John Doe has a plane to catch. Because he's afraid he might be late, he decides to hurry. Tooling along the highway at well over 90 miles per hour in his '66 Renault

Dauphine, a number of interesting things can happen to John Doe.

1. He might make it to the airport in time to catch his flight. No problem. All is well. Driving too fast has been rewarded in this instance.

2. The arresting officer might be in a pretty good mood. Nevertheless, the siren, the flashing red light, and the brief lecture on traffic safety scare the hell out of John Doe, and on top of everything he misses his plane. In this instance, driving too fast has not paid off; it's been punished.

3. The arresting officer might have had a spat with his wife, and now he's in an ugly mood. Consequently, John Doe ends up with a ticket and a court appointment before he can say, "But, Officer—" John will lose $50 and a day of work—and of course, he also misses his plane. Again, the behavior of driving too fast has been punished.

4. John Doe has a bone-jarring collision with a 6-ton truck. For sure, he will miss his plane, and he'll probably miss tomorrow as well. To say that his driving too fast has been punished in this instance would be an understatement.

We have just looked at four possible consequences of driving too fast. The first was rewarding; the other three were punishing. Punishment is simply the opposite of reward. Whereas rewarding a behavior makes it *more* likely to occur again, a punished behavior is *less* likely to recur in the future. Also, just as rewards come in a wide assortment of shapes and sizes, so, too, do punishments. Our beleaguered John Doe was scared, scolded, delayed, fined, and physically injured for speeding. As a result, he will probably think twice before driving so fast again, at least in the immediate future.

Now think for a moment or two about some of the ways children get punished for their misdeeds. Some are scolded; some are spanked; some lose privileges; some forfeit their allowances; some are hollered at; some are sent to their rooms. There is a multitude of ways to punish misbehavior, yet there is one common theme. Punishments are intended to decrease the chances that the misbehavior will happen again.

When Punishment Doesn't Work

You may be thinking right now of how you have repeatedly punished your children for certain things that they do, but somehow they keep right on doing those things anyway. How can that happen? We really don't know the details as to what forms of punishment you use and what behaviors you choose to punish, but we can offer you a few educated guesses.

First of all, there may be a good chance that your child will simply not get caught misbehaving. Children are usually very aware of what behaviors are likely to bring punishment, but they are also very aware of how likely they are to get caught at them. Of course, if they don't get caught, they don't get punished. It's as simple as that. "O.K.," you may be saying, "but what about those things he does right under my nose? He knows I'll notice it and punish him for it, but that doesn't seem to stop him. How do you explain that?" That brings us to our second educated guess. Certain behaviors may have *both* rewarding and punishing consequences. If younger brother has been teasing older brother unmercifully all day long, older brother might suddenly find it very rewarding to land a few punches on him. Even though older brother knows you will punish his fighting, the sheer delight of revenging himself on his younger tormenter, as well as the benefits to his peace of mind for having brought that teasing to a halt, may be well worth the cost of enduring any punishment his parents can hand out to him. In other words, if a behavior continues to occur, despite the fact that it is often and perhaps severely punished, there are probably some powerful rewards serving to maintain that behavior.

Let's look at yet another example of how this works. Little Darlene feels that she hasn't been getting enough parental attention these days. She has tried hard to please her parents, but it seems that they just never notice when she is behaving appropriately. It won't take her long, however, to figure out that misbehavior will get her all the parental attention she can handle. Since negative attention is often better than no attention at all, it won't be surprising if Darlene soon becomes a consistent behavior problem. All this because no one took the time to reward her good behavior with positive forms of attention. You see, kids want their parents to notice them, and, in the long run, most of them would rather be punished than ignored altogether. Our clinic files are filled with cases of children who simply wanted parental attention and resorted to unacceptable means to get it. Many parents don't realize that they have the power to improve relationships with their children simply by effectively giving them attention. In the course of this book, we will show you how you can use that attention in a more consistent and loving way.

Before proceeding further, let's briefly review the material we have covered so far.

1. Behavior is shaped by its consequences, i.e., rewards and punishments.

2. If you'd like to see more of certain behaviors from your child, you have to reward him for engaging in those behaviors.

3. If, on the other hand, you'd like to see less of certain behaviors, you can do one or both of two things:
   a. punish him when he engages in the undesired behavior, or
   b. remove the rewards which have served to maintain the undesired behaviors.

4. When it comes to reward and punishments, remember that no two people are exactly alike in what they value. One child's punishment may be another's reward (remember Darlene?). Be alert for these individual differences.

Problem Definition

Have you ever really thought about *exactly* which of your child's behaviors you'd like to see more or less of? If you are like most parents, you probably haven't. You may know that he's been doing a number of things that annoy you, but have you tuned in *specifically* to what he does that makes you unhappy? Does your child have any particular behaviors that you would like to see less of? For example, does he talk back to you? Does he have tantrums more than you'd like? Would you prefer that he not creep into your bedroom at night quite so often? On the other hand, are there any behaviors in your child's repertoire that give you great pleasure, the only problem being that he rarely engages in them? Would you like to see your child help out more often with the dishes, the yardwork, or perhaps just putting away his toys? Do you wish that he would go along with your requests more often? At any rate, the principles and techniques of behavior change can be successfully applied to a situation only when parents clearly specify for themselves *in detail* the exact nature of that situation. Let's look at an example.

Mr. B. came to us about some difficulties he was having getting along with his nine-year-old son, and some excerpts from our initial interview with him may give you a better understanding of what we mean by specific behavior definition.

> Q: Well, Mr. B., can you tell us a little about what brought you to the clinic today?
>
> A: It's my son, Jeffrey. I've had about all that I can take from him. He's a holy terror, and he's making life miserable for Helen, she's my wife, and me.
>
> Q: A holy terror, uh-huh. What sorts of things has Jeffrey been doing to make you and your wife so upset with him?
>
> A: He's just a godawful brat, that's all. I'm beginning to think he goes out of his way to get us mad at him.
>
> Q: O.K., but can you tell us what you mean by the word "brat"? What makes it seem to you that Jeffrey's a brat?
>
> A: It's simple. He just has a nose for trouble.
>
> Q: O.K., but what does Jeffrey *do* in particular, Mr. B., that gets him into trouble?

A: He fights a lot; it never stops. The house is a shambles. You'd think he'd get tired of it after a while, wouldn't you, Doctor?

Q: Perhaps, but most kids have a great deal of energy, you know. Let me ask you this: Who does Jeffrey usually fight with?

A: Anyone he can get his hands on.

Q: Really?

A: No, I guess that's not true. Come to think of it, he almost always fights with his brother. You know, I sometimes wish he'd fight with the neighbor kids once in a while, just to give his brother a break.

Q: Are there any specific times or occasions when Jeffrey is more likely to fight with his brother?

A: Let's see. . . . I guess it usually happens when Mark, that's Jeffrey's brother, doesn't want to play with Jeffrey any longer. You see, Mark doesn't like to do a lot of the things Jeffrey likes. Mark is a quieter kid; likes to read and build models, you know. Jeffrey, on the other hand, doesn't have the patience to sit around as much as Mark. He likes to run around, play sports, you know.

Q: So can we say that Jeffrey seems like a brat to you because he picks fights with Mark when Mark doesn't want to play with him?

A: Well . . . no, it's not that simple. He also talks back to his mother. I'll tell you one thing, Doctor, if he ever pulled that on me, I'd stop his clock in a hurry.

Q: Are there any particular times or occasions when Jeffrey is most likely to talk back to your wife?

A: Yeah, I guess so. From what she tells me, he sasses her every time she scolds him.

Q: All right. Let's see if we've got the facts straight. Jeffrey has been a problem for you lately for essentially two reasons. First off, he picks fights with Mark when Mark doesn't want to play with him anymore, right?

A: Right.

Q: And second, Jeffrey talks back to his mother when she tries to discipline him. Is that it, or have we left some things out?

A: No, I guess that's it. You know, Doc, when you break it down like that it doesn't seem half so bad, you know what I mean?

Once Mr. B. had defined the situation in terms of specific behaviors, two things happened. First of all, he finally had something concrete to work with. By pinpointing precisely a few undesirable behaviors, he could then proceed with the business at hand, mainly learning and practicing the specific parenting skills he would need to change those behaviors and improve his relationship with his son. Second, did you notice Mr. B.'s comment about the problem not seeming quite so bad any longer? He came into our office that day talking about a brat and a holy terror, but he left with a whole new perspective on his son's behavior. Thus, problem definition in simple and specific behavioral terms not only gives parents something concrete to sink their teeth into—i.e., a few manageable behaviors to work with—but it also shrinks the seeming immensity of the problem. In a sense, it became easier for Mr. B. to see the forest through the trees, and once that happened the forest didn't seem quite so dark and awful anymore. So, if your child is presently engaging in one, two, or even three behaviors which have you crawling the walls, these behaviors may be coloring your perceptions of him and your feelings toward him. Your child is not a "bad" child, and he's not a "good" child either. A child is simply a child, a human being, and although your child may have developed a few behaviors that you are not too happy about, chances are that he or she also says or does a number of things which you appreciate. Part of your job as a parent, then, becomes one of keeping the undesirable behaviors to a tolerable minimum, while at the same time nurturing and rewarding those behaviors which serve to make everyone in your family happier with each other.

What Is Normal?

"But how," you may ask, "are parents supposed to know what is O.K. and what is not O.K.? For instance, every time I try to get Junior into bed before 8 o'clock, he hands me some sob story about how Mrs. Smith down the street lets little Ralphie stay up until 9 every night. Sometimes it makes me wonder if I am being a little too strict." Well, parents are entitled to have differing expectations of their children, as well as different ideas on how to raise them properly. Even the so-called "experts" differ in this respect. Essentially, you must be the judge. *You* have to live with Junior, and *you* are responsible for his health and well-being. Mrs. Smith may also permit Ralphie to sit outside at night and howl at the moon. If she's comfortable with that, great! It's not your problem, nor should her behavior as a parent necessarily be an example for you to follow. Of course, if your neighbors, teachers, or perhaps the police see some of your child's behaviors as decidedly unacceptable, then you might want to reexamine your standards. In general, however, a good rule of thumb to use when considering what to expect from your child's behavior is this: If a behavior is *consistently* annoying you, or *repeatedly* causing you to become angry and upset, do something about it. If you don't, you run the risk of developing a negative attitude about the child. Loving and concerned parents simply cannot afford to let things go that far.

In this chapter we have said that parents should "identify *specific* behaviors," but that can often be difficult to do especially at first. To help you out with this, we've gone through our case files and found some examples of behaviors that have disturbed other parents. Each of these behaviors is specific. If you're really serious about becoming a more effective parent, you might pick out a few of these behaviors and begin keeping a tally or count of how frequently they occur. Some of the behaviors on this list may only occur at specific times; others may occur from morning to night. In any case, start a new tally each day and begin counting—in a week's time you should be able to say with some confidence, for example, that your child has tantrums three to six times per day. By counting behaviors in this way, you will become more sensitive to their frequency of occurrence, as well as more aware of some of the consequences of those behaviors. Perhaps more important, though, you will learn how often a behavior is occurring, as distinguished from simply how annoying that behavior is for you.

Behaviors

Appropriate behaviors that you wish would happen more often:

going to bed on time
proper table manners

hanging up clothes
clearing dishes off the table
brushing teeth
making bed
saying "please" and "thank you"
taking out trash
cooking
planting garden
learning how to care for pets
mowing lawn
completing homework
picking up toys and other play materials

Undesirable behaviors that you would like to have happen less often:

getting out of bed repeatedly before going to sleep
saying "I can't do it," "I know I'll get it wrong"
thumb (finger) sucking
playing in street
throwing food at table
not eating
noncompliance with parental requests
dawdling when dressing
tantrums in public, tantrums at home
running away from home; not coming directly home after
   school
coming into parent's bed at night
interrupting others' conversations
interrupting family members while they're telephoning
hitting, yelling, fighting
shouting
swearing
"talking back"

3 ⋲§ ¿⋺

Social Reward:
The Art of Effective Praising

When to Reward

In Chapter Two, we emphasized the importance of tuning in to your child's behavior. Only when you closely observe his behavior can you determine exactly what he does or doesn't do. We also pointed out that before you can punish your child, you generally need to catch him in the act of misbehaving. The same principle applies to rewards. Before you can reward your child for behaving appropriately, you have to "catch him being good," and this is generally not as easy as it sounds. Misbehavior tends to attract more parental attention than appropriate behavior, and for some very good reasons.

Breaking things, having tantrums, disobedience, and whining, for example, are very intrusive behaviors. They impinge upon your serenity and usually distract you from whatever you happen to be doing at the moment. When your child misbehaves, you generally have to drop whatever you are doing to deal with this misbehavior. Anyone who has ever tried to relax for a few moments with the newspaper after a hard day's work should know what we mean. It's hard to concentrate on the editorial page while your children are squabbling loudly over which TV program to watch. Appropriate behavior, on the other hand, tends not to be such a powerful attention grabber. It usually does not intrude upon your activities. You don't have to drop whatever you are doing to deal with it. Let's suppose, for a moment, that your children happen to be playing quietly while you're reading the paper. What are the chances that you won't even notice them? Since all is quiet, most parents would probably grab at this opportunity for a few uninterrupted minutes of pleasurable activity. If your household is like most households, however, your children will not really know how much you appreciate this good behavior, and you may not realize it either, unless you pause for a few moments to really think about it or it's pointed out to you by someone else.

The explanation for this state of affairs is really quite straightforward. As a rule, most parents simply have not been formally instructed about *when* to reward their children. Almost all parents recognize and reward their children for such extra special things as creativity, perseverance, unusually good manners, high grades in school, and so on, but not many parents really pause to notice and comment upon such simple everyday things as cooperation, doing chores, sharing toys, and so forth. Parents often come to *expect* certain things of their children. Certain forms of good behavior are taken for granted, and as such, not properly rewarded often enough. As a parent, you have the responsibility to teach your children what to do, and not merely what not to do. If you scold your children for disobedience, that teaches them what *not* to do. But this does not really help them to learn what *to* do instead. If you want to see more of certain behaviors from your children, you have to reward them for engaging in those behaviors. In short, it's O.K. to punish your children for disobedience, but it also is of paramount importance, then, that you notice and reward them when they obey.

Don't take any behavior for granted. If your children are entitled to punishment for misbehavior, they are just as entitled, if not more so, to praise when they behave appropriately. How many marital spats, for example, originate because one spouse takes the behavior of the other for granted? Whether it be cooking a nice meal or saying "I love you," these behaviors simply cannot be taken for granted. They need to be rewarded, or they'll soon begin to fade away. Consider for a few moments to what extent you take certain positive behaviors of other family members for granted. You might be surprised.

Before you start feeling guilty or neglectful, and labeling yourself a bad parent, however, we'd like to remind you again that failure to reward positive behavior is a *very* common practice. You're not alone, and our research data bear this out. Before enrolling in our parent workshop program at the clinic, we typically require parents to role-play some standard, everyday situations requiring the use of effective parenting skills. We describe a situation to the parents and then ask them to respond to the children in the situation as best they know how. One of the "reward scenes" reads this way: "Marcia, your typically rambunctious seven-year-old, has been playing quietly and happily with her paints for the last several hours. What would you do?" The principles of behavior change say that a little parental recognition or praise will go a long way toward maintaining or even increasing the probability that Marcia will play quietly like this in the future, yet almost 50 percent of our parents ask Marcia if anything is wrong, suggest that she play outside, or else ignore her altogether. At the conclusion of parent training, however, 100 percent of our parents reward Marcia's behavior with attention and lots of praise. In short, they have learned *when* to reward. The moral is this: Don't get yourself caught in the role of fireman. Practice responding to the nonfires, as well as the fires.

Expecting Too Much Too Soon

Another common trap which parents can easily fall into is saving rewards only for perfect performances. The problem with this is that for many children perfect performances are hard to come by. If your children have grown accustomed to misbehaving most of the time, they are probably not going to turn into perfect angels overnight. If you wait until they do become perfect angels before you reward them, chances are that you may have to wait a long, long time. Remember that behavior is *shaped* by its consequences, and this is usually a gradual process. Major changes do not occur overnight, so be patient and reward your child's efforts to please, even if they aren't perfect. Your child's first attempt at making his bed, for example, might turn out to look like a relief map of the Rocky Mountains. Yet this is a well-intentioned attempt to please you, and, as such, it deserves your appreciation. Effective parents aren't stingy with their praise and encouragement. Let the child know how much you appreciate his helping you out. Later on, you might even ask him to assist you in smoothing out the bumps and wrinkles, and in this way you can help him to learn how to make that bed look even neater. Your first priority, however, is to make the activity pleasant for him and worth his while. When you really stop and think about it, this strategy works for just about every behavior from bed-making to playing tennis to displaying good table manners. To learn anything properly, we need constant feedback along the way to tell us how we're doing. If a child is just starting to learn how to behave in ways more pleasing to you, let him know that he's on the right track. He'll want to hear that, and he'll probably work even harder at it in the future as a result.

The Personal Touch

For most of us, the word "reward" has material or tangible connotations. If Johnny is a good boy, he can have an ice cream cone as his reward. Bring 'em back, dead or alive, and collect a $500 reward from the sheriff. The employer rewards the extra-industrious employee with a cash bonus or a paid vacation in Hawaii. Returning lost jewelry, wallets, or pets to their rightful owners often brings monetary rewards. In short, when we think of rewards, most of us first think of tangible payoffs, and unfortunately this emphasis can be detected in many, if not most, of the traditional behavioral approaches to child management. True, you can change your child's behavior by rewarding him with money, special privileges, tasty snacks, and the like, but there is a much simpler, less expensive, and more loving way that has often been overlooked. That involves simply investing your own time and energy to let the child know that you really appreciate what he's doing. This is the stuff that builds solid parent-child relationships. An example will show you what we mean.

Mrs. G. came to the clinic for some advice. According to her, her son Terry simply wouldn't take responsibility for picking up after himself. No matter how much she pleaded with him, Terry habitually left his toys and clothes lying around on the floor. His bedroom, in particular, was always a disaster area, and Mrs. G. was beginning to get a sore back from having to bend over so often. In short, Terry was behaving like a slob, and his mother was beginning to get pretty upset with him. Terry was getting tired of her nagging. Both were unhappy, and both wanted to see some changes.

In our initial interview with Mrs. G., she suggested that some kind of home program that allowed Terry to earn rewards for being neat might be the answer. We agreed with her. She also stated that she probably would need our help in setting up such a program. Again, we agreed with her. It soon became clear, however, that Mrs. G.'s idea of a home program was rather different from ours. She had been thinking of a program whereby Terry might earn points for appropriate behavior and then cash in these points for money and special privileges. We knew that an approach such as this would probably work, but we also felt it to be somewhat impersonal and unwieldy. So we spent the rest of the session with Mrs. G. turning her on to the concept of social reward. Once she had practiced and mastered the techniques of when and how to praise her son, her problem began to disappear. What's more, she applied her new knowledge to other areas of her life and has reported having great success. Best of all, though, Terry and Mrs. G. are a lot happier with each other now, and isn't that the ultimate goal of any loving parent?

Praising a child for appropriate behavior may at first seem like a simple-minded solution to a problem. The fact of the matter, however, is that it *works*. As we mentioned in the last chapter, parents have a powerful tool for relationship building at their disposal, but most are simply not aware of this. Concerned parents can work wonders just by learning how to distribute their attention systematically, and that's what these parenting skills are all about.

The Advantages of Social Rewards

So what makes social rewards so much better than tangible rewards? First of all, your attention is inexpensive. Tangible rewards cost money, as well as the time and effort that goes into purchasing them. Second, social rewards are portable. They go with you wherever you go, and they are ready to use in virtually any situation you might encounter. You can notice and praise good behavior right on the spot just as it happens. You can carry a sack full of toys, candy, or gold stars around with you, but this gets tiresome after a while. Remember, you're raising a child, not training a dog. Dogs will do tricks for dog biscuits, but children are people, and you'd be amazed at how much they will do for just a few kind words from you. We found there is no quicker, easier, or more human way to build positive family relationships. Rewarding your child's behavior with positive social interaction will create a warmer relationship between the two of you. The more nice things you say to him, the more he'll get your message that you really love and appreciate him. Tangible payoffs and special privileges cannot offer as much, and you will feel better knowing that you are not "buying" good behavior from your child. Instead, he will want to behave in more constructive ways, and all because you have taken the time to recognize and praise him for his efforts. In sum, you'll grow closer to your child, and that's really something worth working toward.

How to Socially Reward

In the beginning of this chapter, we pointed out that most parents do not really know when to reward their children, and we had some research evidence to back this up. The same holds true for the "how" of reward. Without realizing it, most of us are often rather inept when it comes to praising others. We may think we know how, but there's a lot more to it than meets the eye. The art of praising is the most important of all the parenting skills. There are seven basic ingredients or components of praise, and each deserves detailed examination and comment in its own right. We will look at them now one by one, and highlight for you exactly what goes into making praise truly effective.

1. *Look at Your Child*

    The first component of praise is really rather elementary, but you'd be surprised at how often it's neglected. Before you can praise a child effectively, you have to look at him. So what's so earthshaking about that? Well, have you ever tried to have a conversation with someone who either can't or won't look you in the eye? It's downright disconcerting. The message conveyed is that the person isn't really talking with *you* or to *you*. Instead, the conversation tends to have a rather impersonal quality about it. In the same vein, if you praise your child without looking at him, he'll perceive that praise as a perfunctory and perhaps meaningless exercise on your part. You want him to know that you're talking to *him* in particular. Expend the ounce of energy it takes to face your child squarely, and turn your entire body towards him. A sideways glance just won't be as personal or effective. Remember that you are using praise as a reward for his behavior. Make that praise mean something special to your child.

2. *Move Close to Your Child*

Physical proximity substantially increases the power of praise. If you don't believe it, try this simple experiment. Have your spouse sit at the opposite end of the living room from where you are sitting, and ask him or her to say something nice to you. Then ask him or her to come over to where you are sitting and repeat those very same words. We guarantee that you'll be able to feel the difference. Close-up praising is so much more personal and intimate. Your child also feels that difference when you praise him at close range. Even something as simple as a "thank you" is enhanced by physical proximity. So get close to your child—literally—when you praise him; it will really pay off for both of you. This may sometimes mean that you'll have to track him down in another room or even out in the yard. Do it. It's worth the extra effort.

3. *Smile*

How many of us are really aware of the messages we can communicate to others via our facial expressions? And furthermore, how many of us realize that our facial expressions can give messages that are incongruent with what we happen to be saying at the time? Think of the ambivalent father who has been asked by his wife to punish their child for something Dad deep-down believes to be rather cute or clever. Chances are that the child will be more tuned in to Dad's bemused facial expression than to the verbal content of the scolding. At best, the child will be confused by the mixed message. You can give your child this same kind of mixed message if you don't smile when you praise him. A lot has been written about the potency of the smile in winning friends and influencing people. Sometimes just a smile is rewarding enough by itself to make another person feel good, so you can just imagine how powerful a smile can be when it's coupled with lots of praise. When you want to give your child the message that he's pleasing you, make sure your facial expression is giving him that same message.

4. *Say Lots of Nice Things to Your Child*

For most of us, the word "praise" simply means *saying* something nice to another person, but as we have tried to show you here, praise is really more complex than that. Choosing just what to say, however, is still a very important consideration. All of us can easily fall into the habit of saying the same old things every time we praise someone. It can become automatic, for example, to say "Thank you" or "That's nice" or "Good job" or whatever other phrase or set of phrases we happen to habitually use. Just as a baseball pitcher needs to mix his pitches in order to remain effective, so, too, must a parent. Try to recall some of the nice things that people have said to you, some of the compliments that have made you feel really special. You may even want to jot down some of those phrases and begin using them in your everyday conversations with your children. In short, varying the verbal content of your praising will make you seem that much more spontaneous and caring. We have included here a sampling of phrases you might want to consider.

What Do You Say When You Praise?

I like it when you _____.
Good thinking!
Thank you for bringing _____.
You did it!
I'm pleased.
Good work.
That pleases me.
Right.
Why don't you show that to your father, I think he'll be happy.
(Said to a friend of yours in Jimmy's presence:) "Jimmy gets right down to work after school, and his homework is already done."
Good.
You did that right.
Great!
Let me see you do it again.
That's really interesting.
You've really been working hard.

In addition to the specific verbal content of their praising, parents also need to consider *how much* to say when they praise. In a nutshell, you

really can't say too much when you're praising
your child. Remember, your praise and attention
are your child's reward for pleasing you with his
behavior. It is up to you to make sure that it is
substantial enough to make him want to please
you like that again in the future. So make a big
deal out of it. Shower your child with attention,
and say lots of nice things to him. There is a
qualitative difference between saying "Thank
you" and saying "Thank you, it makes me so
happy when you help me out like that." If your
child's behavior is worth praising, it's worth
praising well.

5. *Praise Behavior, Not the Child*
One very important word of caution is in order.
Be sure to praise *behavior*, and not the child. In
other words, praise your child for what he has
done, not what he is. There's a world of difference, for example, between saying "It was nice
of you to help me do the dishes, Diane" and
saying "You are such a good girl, Diane." The
first conveys the message that Diane earned praise
for her behavior, i.e., washing the dishes. The
second statement is merely an opinion about
Diane as a person and does not give her any information as to what she did to merit that high
opinion. In short, tell your children why they
are being praised. Only then can they learn to
discriminate which of their behaviors you find
most positive.

Aside from conveying little or no information
to your child about behavior, praising via phrases
such as "nice boy" or "good girl" poses another
danger. You probably don't want your child to

start believing that he's a "good" child simply because he engages in certain behaviors which are pleasing to you. In the same vein, your child is not a "bad child" simply because he misbehaves. As we pointed out in Chapter 1, your child is neither "good" nor "bad"; he's simply a child.

We've all run across the "high-achieving" personality. He gets his goodies from engaging in certain behaviors and then basking in the limelight while others tell him how "bright," "hardworking," or "talented" he is. His entire self-concept is based on what others tell him, and he knows that if he does certain things other people will label him as a "good" or "fine" person. The only problem with being a high-achiever, however, is that he can never let up. He feels unsure about himself when he's not being told how great he is. Underneath all of his success, then, usually lies an individual plagued by insecurity and self-doubt. In a sense, his self-esteem hinges precariously on the reactions of others to his behavior. You can probably guess where this all got started. As a child, his parents and teachers praised *him*, and not his *behavior*. He was called a "good boy" only when he behaved in certain ways, and probably labeled a "bad boy" whenever he got out of line a little.

Don't label your child because of what he does. He has got to know for sure that in your eyes he is a "good boy" and that you love and respect him regardless of what he does. Praise is simply a technique for letting him know what he does that you appreciate. If you use praise responsibly in this way, he'll grow up not only with a more solid and secure self-concept, but also with a clearer understanding of which of his *behaviors* you find desirable. This may be a somewhat different approach than you're used to, but with a little practice it will quickly become second nature.

6. *Be Physically Affectionate*
It's become very popular these days to talk about body language, and for a good reason. What we do with our bodies, whether it be the way we stand or how we move our arms and legs, says a lot to other people about how we feel about them. We have already discussed how much a simple thing as a smile can enhance the power and credibility of your praise. Well, the same goes for positive body language. A hug, a kiss, or a hand on the shoulder will go a long way toward making your praise something really warm and special to your child. Don't be afraid to show your affection. Get physical with your child when you praise him. Psychological research shows that even such fundamental nonverbal forms of praise as a pat on the head or touch on the arm are very rewarding to children. Just think how much more powerful a hug, coupled with lots of verbal praise, must be. With only the minimal effort it takes to put your arm around your child, you can virtually double the impact of your praise. Fathers shouldn't neglect this with their sons either. Although their behavior may look more like locker-room swats and punches, it's still a rewarding form of interaction for most boys. You communicate your approval and enthusiasm through your body language. If you aren't at all

sure about this, consider for a moment just how nice it feels when your spouse gives you a hug or a kiss. It only makes sense to treat your child the same loving way.

7. *Immediate Reward*

To be maximally effective, reward must be delivered almost immediately upon recognition of the desirable behavior. If you've "caught" your child cleaning up his room, for example, praise him right away. Don't save it for later in the day, or even five minutes later. Research evidence indicates that people learn best with immediate feedback and reward. If you wait too long to reward, it will be more difficult for your child to make the connection between his behavior and the praise. We have found that if you praise within 5 seconds of catching your child being good your praise will be that much more effective. Immediate praise lets your child know right away how you feel about what he's doing, and in that way, his learning is enhanced. Remember, parents are teachers, and their job is to instruct their children in more positive ways of behaving. Immediate reward is essential to this process.

Putting It All Together

The art of effective praising may now seem a bit more complicated than you had originally imagined. We have given you a lot of material to think about and remember, so let's spend a moment here in review and try to tie it all together in one package. Briefly, the seven basic components of praise are:

1. Look at your child
2. Move close to your child
3. Smile
4. Say *lots* of nice things to your child
5. Praise *behavior*, not the child
6. Be physically affectionate
7. Praise the behavior immediately

Each of the above components magnifies the impact of praise on a child. Sure, there will be times when it will be virtually impossible for you to use all seven. Just do the best you can in those situations. We guarantee that once you have mastered the art of effective praising, however, you'll quickly discover the power of praise as a builder of more loving family relationships.

Practice Makes Perfect

Anyone who does anything well probably got there by practicing. There are no shortcuts to skill-building. Just as athletes, musicians, surgeons, and plumbers learn best by doing, so, too, do parents. Consequently, we have incorporated this notion into our parent training package. Supervised practice in the form of *role-playing* has proven again and again to be an exceptionally effective and exciting way for people to master parenting skills. We have research data which show our role-playing methods to be far superior to more traditional parent training approaches. Parents who learn these skills via role-playing become much more adept in their use than parents who simply read and/or discuss the same material. What's more, the role-playing seems to enhance their enjoyment of the whole learning process. The point of all this is simple, yet of vital importance to you. You can get some good things out of this book just by reading it. You can almost double your effectiveness with these techniques, however, if you actively practice them. The choice, of course, is yours, but we can't say enough about the value of learning by doing.

The Role-Play Format

Through our experience with parent training, we have hit upon a standard role-playing format which seems to best meet the needs of parents for serious skill training, as well as enjoyment. It may seem to you at first that a role-play format might lead to mechanical or artificial parenting. Don't worry. With a little bit of practice, parents soon learn to integrate all of the skill components into their day to day parenting behavior without even pausing to think about every little thing they do. In short, effective parents can retain their spontaneity and loving manner by practicing these skills until they are second nature. Look at it this way: If you want to praise your child and make him feel good, you might as well do it the best way possible. Otherwise, the child is merely being cheated out of what he deserves, i.e., his parents' best efforts. Now here is what this role-playing is all about.

Step 1: *Taking Roles*: One parent is designated to play the part of "child"; the other takes the role of "parent."

Step 2: *Setting the Stage*: A scene is read, which describes a typical situation calling for parents to exercise certain parenting skills. A sample scene calling for parental praise, for example, might read something like this: "When you walk into your daughter's bedroom, you are somewhat surprised to find her hard at work on some math problems. What would you do?" At this point, the person designated to play the role of "child" assumes a position consistent with the studying behavior described in the scene. He or she might sit down at a table, for example, and begin pretending to be working on a homework assignment.

Step 3: *Begin Role-Playing*: Now that the stage has been set, the "parent" can begin to role-play praising his or her "child." Let's suppose, for example, that the "parent" immediately walks over to the "child," looks her square in the eye, and says with a smile, "What a good girl—you're doing your homework. Keep up the good work." That ends the role-play, but there's more to this procedure than just that.

Step 4: *The Critique*: The critique may well be the most important part of the entire process. It is at this point that the "parent" receives constructive feedback on his or her performance. Immediately following the role-play segment, the person playing the role of "child" rates the quality of the "parent's" praise, using a 7-point checklist as a guide. The scoring for this sample performance would look something like this:

☐ look at child
☐ physical proximity
☐ smile
☐ positive verbal statement

☐ praise behavior, not child
☐ physical affection
☐ immediate reward

Now let's take a closer look at what happened during the role-play, so we can better understand how it was scored. First of all, the "parent" looked at the "child" squarely. Hence, he or she gets credit for the first component of praising. The "parent" also moved close to the "child" (physical proximity), smiled (smile), said something nice to the "child" (positive verbal statement), and started to praise immediately (immediate reward). This "parent" made two errors, however. First, he or she said, "What a good girl!" Now that is an example of praising the *child*, so credit is not given for "praise behavior, not the child." In addition this "parent" did not touch the "child" at all, thus losing credit for "physical affection." The critique, then, provides an opportunity for the "parent" to find out what he or she did correctly, as well as what components he or she omitted or performed incorrectly. In addition, concrete suggestions as to how the "parent's" performance can be improved are offered and discussed. This feedback is essential to helping parents become more aware of their own behavior.

Step 5: *The Instant Replay*: Once the performance of the "parent" has been properly critiqued and discussed, then it is imperative that the role-play scene be repeated. This not only provides more practice for the "parent," but it also affords him or her an opportunity to make use of the constructive feedback in another scene. Let's see how our "parent" does on the second time around. This time the "parent" walks over to the "child," looks her square in the eye, and says with a smile, "It makes me so happy when you work hard on your homework. Keep up the good work." Then he or she gives the "child" a hug and a kiss. End of scene; a perfect performance.

Step 6: *Critique of the Instant Replay*: This time the "parent" received credit for every item on the checklist. Instead of calling the "child" a good girl, the "parent" let the "child" know how good the "child's" behavior made him or her feel. Also, the hug and kiss more than satisfied the requirements for the "physical affection" item. Here is an example of how practice makes perfect. By combining role-play with constructive feedback and an instant replay, this parent demonstrated mastery of the art of effective praising.

Here are several "sample" scenes for you to practice the art of praising. Role-play these situations with your spouse and/or friends, making sure that you follow the previously outlined format. The components of praise are listed below each scene to serve both as a guide and a scorecard. If you have no one to practice with, you'll simply have to practice in "real-life" situations, and then score your own performance. Be honest with yourself, though. Don't give yourself credit for a praise component that an outside observer might not have noticed. Above all, practice each scene until you have mastered this primary parenting skill.

Practice 1

Your son wanted a puppy—so you bought him one. Just as you predicted, however, he quickly got into the habit of "forgetting" to feed it. But, lo and behold, he has just fed the puppy without being asked. What do you do?

- ☐ look at child
- ☐ physical proximity
- ☐ smile
- ☐ positive verbal statement
- ☐ praise behavior, not child
- ☐ physical affection
- ☐ immediate reward

Practice 2

Your three-year-old's habit of just helping himself to what's in the refrigerator irritates you to no end. He has just asked you for a carrot. What do you do?

- ☐ look at child
- ☐ physical proximity
- ☐ smile
- ☐ positive verbal statement
- ☐ praise behavior, not child
- ☐ physical affection
- ☐ immediate reward

4 ❧ ❧

Effective Limit-Setting

So FAR we have focused primarily on the importance of "catching" children when they're being good and then praising them for their constructive behavior. By no means, however, do we mean to imply that that is all there is to effective parenting. As every parent knows from personal experience, kids will be kids. No matter how often or how lavishly they are praised, all children are bound to misbehave now and then. Periodic misbehavior is a fact of life in all families. Effective limit-setting therefore becomes a useful, if not necessary, parenting skill. How would you respond, for example, to the following situations?

1. Your kids are calling each other names, and you just know an all-out fist fight is right around the corner.
2. Your son has been whining for candy for the last five minutes, even though you've told him you don't have any.

3. Your daughter says "No!" when you ask her to get dressed.

4. Your children ignore your repeated requests to come inside the house for dinner.

Would you ignore the behavior of these children and just hope that it goes away? Many parents do just that, and for some, this approach is very successful. This is especially true in families where misbehavior is the exception rather than the rule. For these lucky parents, limit-setting never really becomes an issue. On the other hand, perhaps you are more inclined to reason with your children about their misbehavior. Some parents are very effective at setting limits in conflict situations simply by showing a lot of affection and understanding toward their children. They may elect, for example, to pick up a four-year-old who has just screamed himself purple in a tantrum, cuddle him in their lap until he quiets down, and then try to reason with him about his behavior. The reasoning might go something like this: "I understand how you might be upset, but next time you want something, please come and whisper in my ear. I'll try my best to help out. I can't promise anything, but I'll sure try. You know, when Daddy or I want something real badly, even though we know we can't have it, we don't lie on the floor and scream about it. We know that we can't always have everything we want the minute we want it. Just remember, we're a family. We love you and we know that you love us. If you get hurt, it's all right to scream. But if you want to talk to me, please do it quietly. That would make me very happy, and like I said, I'll try to help out the best I can."

Still other parents may choose to respond to these kinds of situations with a good deal of firmness. A few quick words to the child and a swat on the rear are not at all uncommon, and many parents swear by this approach.

The point we are trying to make here is simply this: We recognize that limit-setting can be accomplished in a variety of ways. We know that good parents must be flexible and spontaneous enough to respond to their children in ways which take into account the temperament of the child, the personality of the parent, and the circumstances surrounding the particular situation. Of course, we heartily recommend measures that derive naturally out of love for children, but we respect the rights of parents to deal with their children's behavior in the fashion they feel most comfortable with and deem most effective.

The only problem with all this, however, is that not all parents are successful, and, as we mentioned earlier in this book, *repeated* misbehavior and *repeated* negative interactions can have powerful and far-reaching consequences on the quality of family life. Ineffective limit-setting can lead to a great deal of parental frustration and anger. It's not uncommon, for example, for loving parents to actually dislike their kids at times. In addition, without proper limits it is often more difficult for a child to learn constructive behavior. Well-meaning but overly permissive parents, for example, may inadvertently be teaching their children that they don't have to cooperate if they don't feel like it. In short, these parents are training their kids to be less than responsible. Finally, we have seen family situations in which inconsistent and ineffective limit-setting has served to make children anxious and insecure. Children want and need to know just what is expected of them. Children naturally love their parents, so it's really not too surprising that they naturally want to please them. When viewed in this light, parents who effectively set and enforce limits on their children's behavior are simply doing them a favor in the long run. The question, then, is not whether limit-setting is desirable or necessary, because *it definitely is*. The real question becomes one of *how* to set limits in a consistent and loving way, so as to best enhance the child's development while at the same time contributing to everyone's enjoyment of the family experience.

Limit-Setting and the Punishment Equation

For many parents, limit-setting is almost synonymous with punishment. Now we won't argue that punishment may often be needed to enforce household rules, but we do take issue with the popular notion of what punishment really is. Basically, the layman's concept of punishment might best be represented by this simple equation: Punishment = Pain.

The pain in this equation can be either physical or psychological in nature. Your basic garden-variety spanking is probably the most obvious example of physical pain being used as punishment for misbehavior. Psychological pain, on the other hand, can be meted out in a variety of ways. Scolding children, sending them to their rooms, or taking away privileges or allowances are a few of the tried and true methods for making children unhappy, i.e., psychological pain. There is another aspect of the "punishment = pain" equation, however, which is often overlooked. Inflicting pain on children is usually painful for the parent. How often has your child heard,

"This is going to hurt me a lot more than it'll hurt you," or something on that order? You see, pain-producing punishment has this knack of making everyone unhappy, and, worse yet, it often doesn't do any good. All that unhappiness and no guarantee of any behavior change; it hardly seems worth it! Yet the "punishment = pain" equation has thrived for centuries and regrettably will probably continue to do so.

The major shortcoming of the "punishment = pain" concept is that it is an incorrect and misleading definition of punishment. Remember how punishment was defined in Chapter Two? Punishing consequences decrease the likelihood that the punished behavior will occur again in the future. That's a statement about behavior change, and not about pain. In short, punishment does *not* have to cause physical or psychological pain. It simply must decrease the likelihood of subsequent misbehavior. As a parent, you are probably all too familiar with the ineffectiveness of yelling, scolding, and even spanking. A good spanking may stop Junior from beating up on his little brother right then. But will he be less likely to misbehave that way again as a result of that spanking? Maybe and maybe not. *Mild social disapproval* is a useful punishment technique that causes no pain to anyone, yet is remarkably effective as an agent of behavior change.

Mild Social Disapproval: How to Use It

The real beauty of mild social disapproval lies in its subtlety. The person on the receiving end often does not even realize that he's being punished. It's the least severe of all limit-setting techniques, and, once it's mastered and used effectively, mild social disapproval will serve to nip a lot of potentially troublesome situations in the bud. In a sense, it's almost a preventive remedy, which if properly applied, can save both you and your child a good deal of misunderstanding and unhappiness.

Basically, mild social disapproval is a form of parental attention. It typically takes the form of a brief, nonpejorative, low-intensity verbalization that immediately lets the child know when he is treading on thin ice with you. You may be thinking right now something on the order of "So what! My child knows darn well when he's treading on thin ice with me, and, just to play it safe, I usually let him know what I think about it. The problem is that no matter whether I quietly reason with him or yell at him, he usually keeps right on misbehaving. And now you're suggesting that a 'brief, nonpejorative, low-intensity verbalization' will do the trick. You've got to be kidding!"

We can't blame you if you are a little skeptical. Parents who aren't used to getting positive results even when they holler are usually reluctant to try any "softer" measures. Mrs. N. is perhaps a typical example of a parent who at first found it hard to believe that mild social disapproval wasn't useless.

Mrs. N. came to us with a situation faced by many parents. Her son, Freddy, frequently talked back to her. She had tried reasoning with him, explaining how his behavior was very upsetting to her, but it did no good. Freddy continued his backtalk. Lately, however, she had reached the end of her rope and found herself losing her temper and yelling at him. One day he sassed her, and she slapped him quite hard across the face. Mrs. N. understandably became very upset with herself over this, and soon began thinking seriously about getting some help in dealing with her son's behavior.

When we first proposed the notion of mild social disapproval as a possible solution to her problem, Mrs. N. just laughed. "No way," she said. "It'll never work. You'll see." We convinced her, however, to at least give mild social disapproval a fair trial before discarding it completely. Well, she did, and it paid off. Freddy doesn't talk back anymore. As a result, the mother-child relationship is again a sound and happy one. The key to her success, according to Mrs. N., lay in the fact that we systematically role-played with her the entire procedure. This allowed her to integrate the seven basic components of mild social disapproval into a flexible but effective limit-setting technique. When used with all of its components, mild social disapproval is surprisingly powerful. Mrs. N. became a believer. Here are the seven component parts of mild social disapproval.

1. *Look at Your Child*

   When we talked about praising, we noted the importance of looking at your child. The same principle applies to mild social disapproval. Because this is such a low-intensity form of limit-setting, it is imperative that you catch and hold your child's attention. If you fail to look him square in the eye, the chances of your being ignored are just that much greater. Let him know that you are talking to *him* in particular. Sometimes just looking at your child will be enough to get him to stop misbehaving, and, if he's determined to misbehave, at least make him do it right before your eyes. Most of us can probably recall our grade-school days and how certain teachers could swiftly silence their noisy students simply by looking at them. It took real guts to misbehave when they were watching you. So try to establish eye contact with your child. Then he'll know for sure that you're aware of what he's been doing. You'll stand a better chance of getting his undivided attention.

2. *Move Close to Your Child*

Physical proximity is crucial to successful use of mild social disapproval. Think of all the times you've asked your child to stop misbehaving while being a good distance away from him. How many of those times did he stop doing whatever he was doing right away? Not too many, probably. Now think of how fast he straightened out once he saw that you were walking over to him. By moving toward him, you let him know that you meant business, and now he believed it. Whenever possible, stand close to your child when delivering mild social disapproval. Hollering at your child from another room just isn't effective, and you won't have to raise your voice if you're standing next to him. That alone is worth the extra effort.

3. *Disapproving Facial Expression*

Your facial expression must be consistent with what you say to your child. When you praise your child, a smile is essential. Mild social disapproval, on the other hand, calls for a calm but stern look of displeasure. Again, you want your child to know that you really mean business. We've all known people who could freeze Lake Superior with just one icy expression. You certainly don't have to go that far, even if you could, but let there be no doubt in your child's mind that you don't approve of what he's doing. If you get good at this, chances are you'll eventually be able to straighten out bothersome situations simply by giving a brief "look" of disapproval. Words won't even be necessary. That certainly seems easier than hollering or spanking.

4. *Brief Verbalization*

The verbal component of mild social disapproval should, of course, be disapproving in its content, but it doesn't have to be derogatory or pejorative. Often the most effective verbalizations take the form of simple commands. Instead of calling your child a "naughty girl," for example, simply tell her to clean up the mess she's made or to stop playing with that noisy toy gun. Often, just saying your child's name in a firm tone of voice will be sufficient. If possible, however, avoid threats. They paint parents into corners. If you feel you must threaten, though, make sure nothing is said that you either can't or won't back up. Children will occasionally test the limits set by their parents. Later on, we'll show you an effective technique for handling those situations where you feel your back is up against the wall.

Previously we discussed how parental attention of any kind can be rewarding. We pointed out that many children misbehave simply to get noticed, regardless of the quality of the attention they receive. It is of paramount importance, therefore, that you be brief in your verbalizations when delivering mild social disapproval. Long harangues and protracted scoldings may be rewarding to your child. When we talked about praising, we emphasized the importance of saying *lots* of nice things to the child. A lengthy verbal interaction can be rewarding to most children. In fact, research evidence from both homes and schools shows that almost any verbalizations which exceed three sentences in length stand a good chance of rewarding a child's behavior. In short, too much talk can turn mild social *disapproval* into mild social *reward*. Therefore, be brief and to the point. After all, misbehavior is not the appropriate way for your child to gain your attention.

Right now, some may be thinking, "Be brief. Sure, it's easy for them to say. But every time I try to use this mild social disapproval, my kid somehow manages to draw me into a long discussion with all his protests and excuses. How can I be brief with him?" This behavior is called "wheedling," and some children learn to become experts at it. The best way to avoid being "wheedled" is simply to restate your request, together with an escalation of the disapproving quality of your facial expression and tone of voice. Let's look at an example. You have just asked your eight-year-old son James to take out the trash. He immediately starts to whine, "Aw gee, Mom, I helped with the dishes tonight. Make Donny do it. He never does anything. How come I have to do all the work around here?" James may have a point here, but if you're like most parents, you are probably pretty fair when it comes to dividing up the household chores. Anyway, it won't kill him to take out the trash; it's not that big a chore. At any rate, as a parent you are faced with two choices. You can respond to his whining by answering his questions and explaining your entire system of work allocation, or you can simply walk up to James, put on your "I mean business" face, and softly say "I asked *you* to take out the trash. Please do it!" He should get the message. The trash will go out pronto, and you may have saved yourself five minutes of explanations and listening to lame excuses. If James is audacious enough to persist in his wheedling, however, you might move even closer to him and say, "For the last time, take out the trash. Now!" If this doesn't do the trick, you'll probably have to use a more potent limit-setting technique which we shall be discussing in Chapter Five.

5. *Low-Intensity*

Mild social punishment is essentially a *low-intensity* technique. As such, all verbalizations are delivered in a conversational tone of voice. You have probably realized by now that raising your voice really doesn't do much good. Your kids simply get used to it, and you find yourself having to yell louder and louder simply to get their attention. Try this simple experiment the next time you want your child to do something for you. Go up to him and whisper your request in his ear. You'll be amazed to see that you've got his undivided attention. What's more, he'll probably be more likely to comply with your request. So keep that voice volume down. It'll do wonders for everyone's peace of mind.

6. *Nonverbal Gesture Consistent with Disapproval*

A good speaker uses physical gestures for emphasis. As we pointed out in Chapter Three, body language consistent with the content of your verbalizations substantially enhances the impact of your message. A pointed finger, or a finger held to your lips signifying "quiet" can be very effective in and of themselves in stopping misbehavior dead in its tracks. Coupled with a firm, brief, and direct verbalization, these gestures are doubly powerful. In Chapter Three we encouraged you to show physical affection when praising. Lots of affectionate body contact is very rewarding to most children. For this reason, try to avoid showing too much physical affection to your child when delivering mild social disapproval. If you don't, you may inadvertently reward him for his misbehavior. How many parents pick up their children and hold them while trying to reason with them about their misdeeds? Plenty, and most of them would be quite surprised to realize that such an approach to discipline often increases the likelihood that such misbehavior will occur again in the future. Use physical gestures for emphasis, then, but steer clear of using too much physical contact when you set and enforce limits.

7. *Immediate Delivery*

Mild social disapproval is designed to correct problem situations before they get out of hand. Immediately upon recognizing some misbehavior getting started, use mild social disapproval to keep things under control. Misbehavior typically builds in intensity, gathering force and energy as it grows. A little mild social disapproval used early on can save a lot of problems and headaches for everyone later. An example will give you a better idea of what we mean. John and Mary, your three-year-old twins, are playing quietly with blocks on the living-room floor. Pretty soon you notice that John is getting a little irritated with Mary because she won't share any of the blocks. Shortly thereafter, John starts to holler at Mary and grab up all the blocks he can lay his hands on. Mary doesn't appreciate John's attack, so she clobbers him with one of the blocks. Now the fight is on, and you've got the task of separating two screaming kids. They're all hot and bothered, and by the time you are able to straighten out this situation, chances are that you will be, too. This entire scene could have been avoided, however, simply by setting limits with some well-timed mild social disapproval just as the pot was beginning to boil. A parent who sensed trouble as soon as the kids began to hassle each other about the blocks and then quickly responded with some mild social disapproval could have saved himself, as well as his children, a lot of unnecessary misery. Walking up to Mary, looking her square in the eye, pointing a finger, and saying, "Mary, please share those blocks with John," probably would have been enough to prevent the wild scramble which later ensued. So be quick with mild social disapproval. If you can smell trouble brewing, respond immediately. This may require some practice in terms of learning how to recognize trouble situations early, but as a parent you are probably already rather knowledgeable in this regard. It may sound trite to say that an ounce of prevention is worth a pound of cure, but it really rings true in the realm of child misbehavior.

A Pause to Summarize

Mild social disapproval is a quick and effective way to set limits on your children's behavior, and it saves a lot of wear and tear on everyone involved. Mild social disapproval is composed of seven basic components, each of which contributes to the overall effectiveness of your parenting. These are:

1. Look at your child
2. Physical proximity
3. "Disapproving" facial expression
4. Brief (less than three sentences) verbalization
5. Low-intensity tone of voice
6. Gesture consistent with disapproval
7. Early use of mild social disapproval

Mild social disapproval by its very nature, must be used calmly, smoothly, and quickly in order to be maximally effective.

Following Through

Once you've used mild social disapproval, you've actually done only half the job required for successful behavior change. Punishment teaches a child only what you *don't* want him to do. As we pointed out in Chapter 3, praise is the most effective tool for teaching a child more constructive behavior. As such, it is imperative that you follow all instances of mild social disapproval with a healthy dose of praise *as soon* as your child begins to behave more appropriately. This may be difficult at first, since most parents simply aren't in the habit of praising their children so soon after they have misbehaved. This is the optimal way to instruct your child in more positive behavioral alternatives.

Follow the disapproval sequence with praise as soon as the child begins to behave more appropriately. Keep the following checkpoints in mind.

1. Look at child
2. Get close physically
3. Smile
4. Say lots of nice things to child
5. Praise behavior, not child
6. Show physical affection
7. Make reward immediate

This entire sequence may seem rather long and involved to you. True, it is more complex than simply praising or punishing alone, yet just a little practice on your part is all that's required for mastery of this vital two-stage parenting skill.

When you are dealing with more than one child, mild social disapproval can become a three-step procedure. Let's suppose for a moment that you have just asked your two children, Bob and Ray, to help you with the dishes. Let's also suppose that Bob pitches in enthusiastically, but Ray has ignored your request and continues to play with his toys. What should you do? Well, top priority goes to praising Bob. After all, he responded to your request right away. Step 1, then, involves praising the child who is behaving appropriately. Step 2 consists of giving mild social disapproval to Ray, and this is immediately followed by Step 3, praising Ray as soon as he begins to help out. The entire three-step procedure won't take any longer than 20 seconds, but the results will be truly startling.

To help you practice the mild social disapproval techniques, we have included some more sample scenes which you can role-play. If you need to, review the role-play format outlined in Chapter Three. Again, role-play practice is crucial to your success with these techniques. We guarantee you that a little time spent practicing will pay off handsomely in terms of improved child behavior and family relationships.

Practice 1

While shopping with your six year old, you pass a toy store and he tries to pull you into the store. You assert, "I'm sorry, honey, I don't have enough money for toys today. Let's go." To which he replies "No!" What do you do?

A. Use mild social disapproval for saying "No":
- ☐ look at child
- ☐ physical proximity
- ☐ "disapproving" facial expression
- ☐ brief verbalization (less than three sentences)
- ☐ low intensity
- ☐ gesture consistent with disapproval
- ☐ early use of mild social punishment

B. Then comes the praise portion of the sequence:
- ☐ look at child
- ☐ physical proximity
- ☐ smile
- ☐ positive verbal statement
- ☐ praise behavior, not child
- ☐ physical affection
- ☐ immediate reward

Practice 2

You have asked your two children to help carry the groceries in from the car. Alice pitches in enthusiastically but Jane continues to play with her toys. What do you do?

A. First comes the praise portion of the sequence to Alice:
   - ☐ look at child
   - ☐ physical proximity
   - ☐ smile
   - ☐ positive verbal statement
   - ☐ praise behavior, not child
   - ☐ physical affection
   - ☐ immediate reward

B. Then use mild social disapproval for non-compliance:
   - ☐ look at child
   - ☐ physical proximity
   - ☐ "disapproving" facial expression
   - ☐ brief verbalization (less than three sentences)
   - ☐ low intensity
   - ☐ gesture consistent with disapproval
   - ☐ early use of mild social punishment

C. Then praise Jane for behavior change:
   - ☐ look at child
   - ☐ physical proximity
   - ☐ smile
   - ☐ positive verbal statement
   - ☐ physical affection
   - ☐ praise behavior, not child
   - ☐ immediate reward

When to Use Mild Social Disapproval

Perhaps we might backtrack here for a moment to consider in somewhat more detail just when a parent needs to set limits. As we stated in Chapter Two, it's essentially up to *you*, as a parent, to decide which of your child's behaviors are positive (and thus deserving of praise) and which behaviors are unacceptable to you. Every parent will have his or her own unique notion of just what sort of behavior merits disapproval. Remember, you and your children have to live together. You can help make that a more positive experience for everyone through effective parenting. A loving and concerned parent shows his love by dealing with potentially disruptive family situations in a fair and consistent fashion. Mild social disapproval is exceedingly useful in achieving that end.

From the list of scenes and some of the examples we have presented in this chapter, you now have a pretty good idea of the kinds of problems that are most effectively dealt with by mild social disapproval. It is perhaps most useful for coping with the common everyday refusals to do what is asked. More important, however, mild social disapproval can often be used to prevent minor problems from becoming major ones.

Rules

As long as we're talking about *when* to set limits, and in particular, preventing the occurrence of major problem situations, let's take a few moments to consider the importance of rules in this process. Every household has rules. Don't let anyone tell you differently. In some households, however, it may *seem* as if there aren't any rules, but this is only because the rules are implicit, vague, and constantly changing. The problem with this is that it's not only difficult for the children to know what's expected of them, but it's also just as tough for the parents to know when to reward and when to punish. Rules don't have to be restrictive. In fact, well-made rules can go a long way toward making family members a lot more confident, comfortable, and secure about their behavior. Effective rule-setting is a handy skill, and it is nothing that any parent cannot master with a little thought and practice. Rules guide children in learning what behaviors are desirable, as well as prompting parents to be *consistent* in their responses to their children's behavior. Here are some guidelines for rule-setting.

1. Rules should be short and to the point. If they are, they will be more easily remembered and hence, more likely to be followed.
2. Rules should specify *in detail* the behavior required. If rules are vague, there may be some misunderstandings about if and when a rule has been broken. A clearly stated rule will give you more confidence in your decisions about when to reward and when to punish. Ill-defined rules are difficult to enforce.
3. Rules should be stated *positively*. "Clean your plate before eating dessert," for example, sounds more pleasant and appealing than "You can't have dessert if you don't clean your plate."
4. Start one new rule at a time. Too many rules all at once can be confusing, for parents as well as children.
5. Ask your children to help you make up the rules.

You will be amazed at how fair they can be. What's more, they will be more likely to understand, remember, and follow rules which they helped to develop.

6. Be firm and consistent once the rules have been established. Making exceptions and listening attentively to excuses and protests will only weaken your authority as a parent. Once *everyone* has agreed to a rule, stick by that rule. If it soon becomes apparent that a particular rule is unfair or ineffectual, however, then it is time to sit down with your children and draw up a new one.

Requests

Just as rules need to be clear and direct, so must your requests. Noncompliance with parental requests is a major source of irritation for parents, as well as being the most common of all child behavior problems. If you have to spend a lot of time coaxing and cajoling every time you want your child to do something, the pleasure of life evaporates. Parents can do a lot to avoid this problem simply by altering the nature of the requests they make of their children.

Have you ever asked your child if he'd like to help you clean up or do dishes? If so, what do you do when he says he'd really rather not? You can't get angry with him because he hasn't disobeyed you. He has simply given an honest answer to a somewhat dishonest question. The question is dishonest because "Yes" is the only response you wanted. The child really has no choice, but the indirect and interrogative nature of your request has given him the illusion of choice.

If you want your child to do something for you and you're not going to accept anything less than compliance, you had better *tell* him what you want done. Don't ask a question unless you're fully prepared to live with the answer. Now we don't mean to imply here that parents should run around barking orders like drill sergeants. Telling your child what you want of him need not be harsh or unpleasant. You can smile, say "please," and use a perfectly pleasant tone of voice when you make requests of your children, but they need to know that you expect them to comply.

The second major consideration in making requests is clarity. Be specific. Let's suppose, for example, that your child's whining has finally frayed your nerves. You thus ask him to "knock it off." Now put yourself in your child's shoes. What exactly did you ask him to do? Should he stop whining? Maybe. Should he stop following you around? Maybe. Should he stop breathing? How should he know? Your command to "knock it off" was simply too vague. Not enough information was conveyed. Parental commands should prescribe the specific behaviors required. Wouldn't a command like "Junior, please stop that whining" have been a lot clearer and easier to understand? Now the child knows exactly what you want. There's no room for argument about what you mean if you request *specific* behaviors.

One word of advice before we leave the topic of parental requests. Try not to get into the habit of always telling your child what not to do. If possible, suggest appropriate alternatives for him. For example, instead of simply asking your children to stop wrestling in the living room, you might also suggest that it's all right if they wrestle, provided they do it outdoors in the yard. Providing alternative behaviors helps frame everything in a more positive context, as well as increasing the probability that your requests will be carried out.

Of course, no matter how proficient you become in making requests, there will always be occasions when your children will disobey you. Kids will test you out from time to time. A little mild social disapproval, however, will go a long way toward remedying those situations quickly.

5 ❧ ❧

Time Out

Mrs. P. came to us with a problem. Let's listen in on a taped segment of our initial interview with her and find out what that problem was all about.

Us: Well, Mrs. P., can you tell us a little about what brought you to the clinic?

Mrs. P.: I guess basically the problem is that I can't get Richard, he's my seven-year-old, to obey me. Every time I ask him to do something, no matter what it is, it turns into a big deal, you know what I mean?

Us: Possibly. It would be helpful if you would give us an example of what you mean.

Mrs. P.: O.K., let's say I ask him to turn off the TV and come into the kitchen for lunch. He'll just say "No!" Right to my face. Now should I have to stand for that?

Us: Well, it's apparent that it's upsetting to you when Richard behaves like that. But, tell us, what do you do when Richard says "No"?

Mrs. P.:   Then I might say something like "Richard, I'm warning you," or "You better move or you're in big trouble."

Us: And then?

Mrs. P.:   And then he usually says "So what?" Can you believe it?

Us: Sure. It sounds like he's not particularly afraid of the consequences. How do you back up your warnings?

Mrs. P.:   Well, that's just it. I think he knows that I don't like to spank him, and, to be honest, half the time I just let the whole thing ride. You don't know what a hassle it is to spank that kid. He wriggles and screams the whole time, and I don't even hit him that hard. The worst part, though, is when it's over. He'll start slamming doors and yelling "I hate you!" I know he doesn't mean it, but I don't think any mother likes to hear those things from her kids. And yesterday he took a swing at me, and that's when I decided to get some help with all this.

Us: It sounds like he's been punishing you for trying to punish him.

Mrs. P.:   Well, whatever, I think it's time for some changes, don't you?

Mrs. P. was confronted with a problem that faces most parents at some time or another. The child misbehaves, so the parent asks him to stop. The child continues to misbehave, so the parent threatens dire consequences.

Then, by not heeding this warning, the child forces the parent's hand. Once your child has been warned, you have to back it up. The problem is, however, that many parents find major punishment techniques, like "grounding," yelling, and spanking in particular, rather repugnant. Everyone winds up unhappy. In this chapter, we will outline in detail for you a discipline technique of proven effectiveness. It's called time out, and it works very nicely as a trump card to be played if and when your child openly decides to test your limits.

Physical Punishment: The Pros and Cons

Before we get into the when and how of time out, however, let's take a few moments here to examine the value of spanking and other forms of physical punishment. First of all, physical punishment can be a real hassle for everyone involved. Mrs. P. was a case in point. Tempers often flare up on both sides. What's more, spankings can generate bad feelings between parent and child for hours afterward. True, spanking may make a parent feel a little better right away in that he or she gets the chance to let off some steam, but letting off steam is not the purpose of punishment. Child discipline is only to be used for teaching your child the difference between acceptable and unacceptable behavior. Avoid getting caught in the trap of using physical punishment simply as a means of expressing your anger.

It's not that physical punishment doesn't teach children anything. It's just that it teaches them the wrong things. Psychological research has shown that children can learn simply by observing the behavior of others. What's more, they pay special attention to the behavior of persons they look up to and admire. So, if as a parent you find yourself using physical punishment as a discipline tool, your child is probably learning that aggressive behavior is the preferred solution to problems. There is some evidence to suggest, in fact, that children who come from homes where physical punishment is often used tend to be more physically aggressive with their peers. And that's probably not the best route to getting along with one's schoolmates.

Another problem with physical punishment is that it tends to work only when the punishing agent is around. You can spank the daylights out of your children every time they misbehave, and eventually they will toe the mark for you. But that's just for you and you alone. You've probably encountered a number of families where one parent can command all kinds of compliance and obedience through physical punishment, yet when that parent is not at home the kids run wild. Furthermore, even if both parents happen to be quite effective in dishing out physical punishment, what happens when their child goes to school and is out of their jurisdiction, so to speak? Our files are filled with cases where parents have relied on physical punishment to keep order at home, but their kids became absolute terrors in school as a result.

Finally, parents tend to spank when they're angry. Generally, they are pushed to their limits, lose their tempers, and then take it out on the child in the form of physical punishment. We're not saying that unacceptable behavior doesn't deserve to be punished; it usually does. It's just that when people lose their tempers they often do things that they later regret. How many parents, in a fit of anger, have spanked too hard or sent their children to their rooms for hours? And how many of these parents have later calmed down, only to realize that perhaps they had been too harsh with their kids? It's no fun knowing that you've been too rough with your child. After all, he's your own flesh and blood, and you love him dearly. It hurts to see him hurt, especially by you. Time out is a technique designed to avoid all this hurt, as well as promote constructive behavior change.

Time Out: A Gentle but Consistent Form of Discipline

Children want and need to know where they stand. They prefer reason and order to haphazard discipline and emotional chaos. In fact, there exists a great deal of clinical evidence which indicates that free-floating anxiety and insecurity are frequent derivatives of inconsistent parenting and punishments disproportionate to the behavior. Certainly no loving and concerned parent would wish these things for his children, but love and concern often simply aren't enough. Effective parenting demands the use of *reasonable, fair,* and *consistent* procedures, employed in an overriding context of caring.

Time out was developed primarily with the well-being of the child in mind. It is both physically and psychologically safe, thus allowing parents to be consistent without seeming cruel or inhuman. In sum, not only is time out a proven technique of behavior change, it also works to preserve the positive quality of the parent-child relationship.

Time out is an abbreviated way of saying "time out from a positive reward." We like to think of it as a brief "cooling-off" period. Basically, time out involves placing the misbehaving child, for a short period of time, in a situation in which he receives little, if any attention, as well as few opportunities to engage in any rewarding activities. For years parents have used variations of the time-out procedure, the most common ones being the solitary chair in the corner or sending the child to his room. For the most part, however, these procedures have tended to be used erratically and, often as not, accompanied by heated exchanges between parent and child. Time out, as outlined here, is a planned and systematic alternative to other "hit-and-miss" procedures. Given such a blueprint for effective action, parents can confidently discipline their children without the fear of being too lenient, too harsh, or saying things that they really don't mean. And when it's all said and done, it's the children who benefit most from clearly defined and consistently enforced behavioral expectations.

The Rationale for Time Out

As we see it, time out serves three useful functions. First of all, time out serves to terminate problem situations quickly, thus preventing further escalation. If you notice that your children are fighting, for example, swift use of time out can do much to prevent further bodily injury or property damage. Second, as we mentioned earlier, it provides a brief "cooling-off" period, giving both parent and child time to settle down and regain control of their emotions. As a result, each will be less likely to say or do something which he will later regret. Finally, time out gives the child several minutes, free from distractions, to think about the way he has been behaving. This fact alone makes future behavior change much more probable. Of course, parents, too, can use this time to think about their behavior, or, more specifically, how they're reacting to the child's behavior.

All in all, the consistent use of time out can inject some sanity and reason into otherwise highly charged and emotional situations.

As such, we recommend time out to be used specifically for high-intensity problems, such as fighting, destructiveness, throwing tantrums, and the like. Looking at the role-play scenes presented in this chapter will also give you a better idea of what types of situations are best neutralized by time out.

Perhaps the nicest thing about time out is that it provides a back-up to your warnings. You no longer have to issue idle threats and then suddenly find yourself backed into a corner. Time out also puts more power into mild social disapproval. The child soon learns that you mean to be consistent, that you're ready to enforce your requests with a time out, if necessary. We cannot emphasize enough the importance of being consistent and following through. When a rule is broken, you simply have to enforce it; otherwise, why have rules at all? If you don't, your children will quickly realize that you're just a paper tiger, an old softie who can be manipulated at their pleasure.

One word of caution is in order, however, before we leave the topic of time out. Time out is a parent's trump card; don't overplay it. In other words, don't start putting your children in time out for every kind and sort of misbehavior. Instead, save it for major, high-intensity and highly disruptive behaviors. Mild social disapproval can handle the smaller stuff quite well.

The Need for a Rule

Rule-setting is an essential part of the time-out procedure. Since time out is a tool for teaching your child, clearly defined and enforceable rules can aid you in that process. Stating the rule each time it is broken is also helpful, as it serves as a useful reminder to your child. If you need some help in formulating useful and well-defined rules, refer back to Chapter Four and reread the section on rule-setting.

In general, we don't recommend using time out for more than one behavior at a time. That is, make only one rule that will be enforced with time out. Of course, your child may regularly engage in several different behaviors that merit time out, but too many rules punishable by time out cause a lot of confusion, both for you and your child. Keep things as simple as possible. Your child will learn more quickly if you do, and that is really what you are after here. You can make your rules very broad, however, broad enough to cover a wide range of situations. For example, you might make a general rule that destroying another's property automatically earns your child a time out. In such cases, all you need to say to your child is, "You deliberately broke Ginger's wagon. For that, you have to go to time out." Now isn't that a little easier on you as well as your child, than going through a long harangue each time the child misbehaves? It also lets your child know in clear and explicit terms exactly why and how he is being punished.

How to Use Time Out

The effectiveness of time out, just like the other techniques presented in this book, depends to a great extent on the manner in which it is employed. And just as we outlined the basic components of praise and mild social disapproval for you in previous chapters, we will here present the four checkpoints essential to the success of the time-out procedure.

1. *Remain Calm*

   Perhaps the most important thing to remember about time out is this: Don't lose your temper. This may be difficult to do at first, but remaining calm and reasonable is crucial to the entire procedure. Psychological research has shown that getting Mom's or Dad's goat can sometimes be quite rewarding for many children. Since you really want to avoid rewarding your child's misbehavior, it makes better sense to remain calm. Don't let your child have the satisfaction of getting a rise out of you. You'll feel better, as well, if you aren't yelling and swinging. The first step to gaining control of any situation is to get your own emotions under control.

2. *State the Rule and the Consequence*

   There are two, and only two, things you need to say to your child when delivering time out. First, remind him of the rule he has broken, and then inform him of the consequences of breaking that rule. For example, you might say, "You've been told before not to scream at your mother. For that you have to go to time out." That's it. Short and sweet. If you say much more than the two sentences about the rule and the consequence, you may end up inadvertently rewarding children's misbehavior with too much of your attention.

3. *Ignore Subsequent Verbalizations*

Once they have been informed that they are about to be punished, children will often try to get out of it by pleading, making excuses, protesting, or even throwing tantrums. Try to avoid getting caught up in a lengthy discussion with your children. Once you've stated the rule and the consequence, do your best to ignore all subsequent verbalizations. Children often test their parents to see if they really mean business. If you start letting your children off the hook by responding attentively to his excuses, all they're going to learn is that, if they break a rule, they will probably be able to talk themselves out of trouble. That kind of learning certainly is not conducive to constructive behavior change. So be prepared to ignore teary-eyed promises that they "won't do it again" or excuses like "Jennifer started it." Time out depends on your being consistent and following through when a rule has been broken.

It is also important that you ignore all verbalizations that your children make while they're *in* time out. Be prepared for statements like "Can I come out now?" or "I hate it in here." These are popular (and often effective) devices to obtain parental attention. If you can ignore them, your time-out program will simply be that much more effective.

4. *Follow Through Quickly*

As soon as you are aware that your children have broken a rule, you must initiate the time-out procedure. As pointed out in the praise and mild social disapproval chapters, we have found that the sooner you respond to misbehavior, the more effective you can be. Now that doesn't mean that you have to hustle your children off to the time-out area in the blink of an eye. It simply means that once you have noticed the misbehavior, you should *begin* the procedure. Again, we have found 5 seconds to be a reasonable amount of time in which to respond. Responding quickly in this way has several advantages. First, it emphasizes for the children the connection between the inappropriate behavior and its punishing consequences. Second, swift use of time out serves to shorten these otherwise aversive or unpleasant situations, thus saving a little wear and tear on everyone involved. If you use time out to deal with tantrums, for example, the faster you can terminate that noisy tantrum, the less frayed your nerves will be. Finally, if you get into the habit of responding quickly to your child's misbehavior, he will soon get the message that you are very aware of what he does and are prepared to act quickly and firmly when the situation requires it.

A Pause to Review

Let's take a minute here to review the four basic components of time out. When delivering time out, parents should:

1. Remain calm
2. Make sure the rule and the consequences have been stated *before* misbehavior occurs. Restate them when the misbehavior takes place.
3. Ignore extraneous verbalizations and excuses
4. Deliver time out quickly

Finally, it is important for parents to remember to praise their children as soon as they begin to behave appropriately following time out. Again, punishment teaches a child only what he is not supposed to do. Praising is the most effective way to teach children more appropriate alternatives. So look for opportunities to "catch them being good." A fast hug and a kiss, for example, followed by "I know you'll try not to scream at Mommy again" will be a powerful demonstration to the children that you still love them and that you aren't bearing any grudges. Everyone will feel better if you do.

If you feel that practice will make you more confident about using the time-out procedure, you'll find a couple of examples to work with on the following pages.

Practice 1

Cynthia and Jan have been told what time out is and that every time they fight they will go to time out. Right now you can hear screaming and yelling in the den suggesting another fight is starting. Soon, Jan appears complaining that Cynthia took Jan's favorite crayons. What do you do?

A. Deliver time out:
   ☐ remain calm
   ☐ state the rule and the consequence

☐ ignore extraneous verbalizations and excuses
☐ follow through quickly

B. Following removal of child from time out, praise:
    ☐ look at child
    ☐ physical proximity
    ☐ smile
    ☐ positive verbal statement
    ☐ praise behavior, not child
    ☐ physical affection
    ☐ immediate reward

Practice 2

Your repeated use of mild social disapproval has not produced results for Ricky's playing with the gas oven. You set up the rule: If you play with the stove, you go to time out. You are just waking up in the morning but you hear Ricky in the kitchen playing with the stove. What do you do?

A. Deliver time out:
    ☐ remain calm
    ☐ state the rule and the consequence
    ☐ ignore extraneous verbalizations and excuses
    ☐ follow through quickly

B. Following removal of child from time out, praise:
    ☐ look at child
    ☐ physical proximity
    ☐ smile
    ☐ positive verbal statement
    ☐ praise behavior, not child
    ☐ physical affection
    ☐ immediate reward

Choosing a Suitable Time-Out Area

Now that you have learned and practiced the effective way to use time out, you may be wondering just *where* to put your child when he misbehaves. As we mentioned earlier, the bedroom may not be an appropriate place, largely due to all the entertaining and rewarding activities available there. The *ideal* time-out area should be free of possibilities for social interaction or rewarding activities. Most homes don't have any such areas, however, so you have to use your imagination in choosing a location that closely approximates the ideal. In our experience, we have found that kitchens, laundry rooms, and the like make reasonably good time-out areas. Kids usually can't have too much fun in those places. If none of these areas is convenient for you, however, you might try a stairwell or even a chair facing the corner in another room. A bedroom might be used, provided it isn't overloaded with books, toys, games, and the like. Again, the idea behind time out is that it gives the child an opportunity to cool off, examine what he's been doing, and consider more appropriate alternatives. If he is distracted from this by extended social interactions or too many other fun things to do, chances are that he might never get around to thinking about his behavior. When that happens, time out becomes no more than a waste of everyone's time. One word of caution, though, in choosing a time-out area. Dark closets and other small, airless rooms are *not* suitable. You don't want any of your children to become claustrophobics simply because they misbehaved a little. Remember, the whole idea behind time out is to discourage misbehavior and encourage more acceptable behavior. The time-out area you choose should be dull enough to teach that lesson, but not so isolated or frightening that it creates far-reaching emotional upset.

Choice of a time-out area will also vary depending upon the age of the child. Placing a misbehaving tot in his high chair for a couple of minutes should serve your purposes well, whereas an older child probably will have to be timed-out in another room. Feel free to experiment a bit at first in order to determine the most suitable time-out location for your child.

How Long Should Time Out Last?

The duration of time out depends, to a great extent, on the age of the child. Two-year-olds, for example, often learn quite well from time outs which last no more than a couple of minutes. Older children, on the other hand, typically need to be placed in time out for somewhere between three and six minutes. You may have to experiment a bit, before deciding on the appropriate length of time. Start small, say two or three minutes, and see if that has any effect on subsequent misbehavior. If it doesn't, you'll need to up the ante a bit, possibly to five or six minutes. Once you have found the appropriate time period, however, stick with it. If you're administering time out for fighting, for example, don't assign three minutes one day for some pushing and shoving, and then turn around the next day and hand out a ten-minute sentence simply because someone got a bloody nose that time. Consistency is the watchword of time out, both in terms of using it *every* time the rule is broken, and in determining how long a time out should last. To help you in becoming more consistent with time out, we recommend that, if you don't have one, you purchase an inexpensive oven timer to remind you and the child when time out is over. If you don't, you may either lose track of the time or else your child may constantly be asking if "time is up yet."

One problem occasionally encountered with time out is the tantrum and other forms of angry resistance. Especially at first, your child may not be very cooperative about going to the time-out area. Don't be alarmed. You are just being tested to see if you mean business. Above all, don't hit him, yell at him, or drag him to the time-out area by his ear. Calmly but firmly take him by the arm and walk him to time out. Also, let him know that if he continues to be disruptive in time out, that time will count as "dead time" and be added on to the time out period. In this way, the child soon learns that there is only one way to get out of time out quickly, and that is to *quietly* sit through the allotted time period.

As you can see, time out is usually over and done with in a few minutes. In fact, you may be wondering how it can work at all, given the limited duration of the procedure. Many parents have grown accustomed to sending their kids to their rooms for hours, and viewed in this context, time out may seem rather innocuous to them. Research evidence indicates, however, that time out is one of the most powerful techniques available for changing behavior. And since it can be carried out so quickly and gently, it spares everyone involved a lot of wasted time, energy, and hard feelings. Parents who previously may have had to rely on yelling and/or spanking now have a brief but effective solution to problem situations.

6 ৶ ৡ

Ignoring

UP TO THIS POINT we have devoted our efforts to showing you just when and how to distribute your attention. By now you should be convinced of the power of parental attention to change children's behavior. In this next chapter, however, we plan to instruct you in the proper procedure for *not* giving your child attention. This is called *ignoring*, and you may be surprised to find out that ignoring a child is not as easy to do as some might believe. If parents use ignoring at the wrong time or in the wrong manner, the consequences can be devastating in terms of child misbehavior. Mrs. T. found this out the hard way.

Mrs. T. had heard from her neighbor that the best way to get a child to stop whining was simply to ignore him whenever he whined. That sounded easy enough to her, so Mrs. T. systematically set about the business of ignoring her constantly whining and complaining five-year-old daughter. Whenever the whining started, Mrs.

T. began to ignore. She stuck with this program for several weeks. It soon became apparent to her, however, that little Linda was still whining and complaining as much as ever. Well, she finally threw in the towel and came to see us at the clinic. She was puzzled and confused, but determined to find out what had gone wrong with her program.

In our initial interview with Mrs. T., we quickly stumbled onto the reason her ignoring had failed. Mrs. T. simply had not been ignoring properly. Whenever Linda started to whine and complain, Mrs. T. took great pains *not* to respond to her—almost. Every couple of minutes, Mrs. T. would remind her still-whining daughter that she wasn't going to speak with her as long as she was whining like that. By repeatedly reminding her child that she was going to be ignored, Mrs. T. had inadvertently sabotaged her entire program. She was, in fact, paying attention to Linda while she whined, and from what you've learned so far, you know that paying attention to a behavior can make it more likely to recur. Once we had pinpointed Mrs. T.'s error and role-played a few ignoring-type situations with her, she was then able to deal more effectively with her daughter's whining behavior. We hope that you will benefit as well from the systematic instruction on ignoring that follows in this chapter.

Why Ingoring Works

The rationale for using ignoring as a behavior change technique is quite straightforward. Much of children's behavior is maintained by the attention it receives. As we pointed out in earlier chapters, even negative forms of parental attention can be rewarding to some children. In a sense, parents who pay a lot of attention to their kids' misbehavior are simply teaching them that misbehavior will be rewarded. By cutting off that supply of attention for misbehavior, ignoring serves to decrease the chances that it will occur in the future.

When to Ignore

It is of the utmost importance that parents learn *when* to ignore their children. Too often parents can fall into the trap of unintentionally ignoring appropriate behavior and responding only to misbehavior. It is crucial, then, that parents attend to and comment upon their children's behavior whenever it is constructive. The question then becomes one of which of your children's misbehaviors are most amenable to change via ignoring. As a general rule, ignoring works best with *persistent* behaviors that are rather obvious attempts to gain parental attention.

One such obvious attention-seeking behavior had been spoiling many an evening for Mr. and Mrs. A. Their 2½-year-old son Robby refused to go to sleep at night without one of his parents in his bedroom. Unless someone was with him each night, Robby would cry and holler from his bed, thus making any reading, TV viewing, or conversation almost impossible for Mr. and Mrs. A. They had tried several times to wait him out, hoping against hope that Robby might simply cry himself to sleep. Sooner or later, however, they would be so moved by his apparent distress that one of them would go into his room to calm him down. What they were really teaching

Robby through all this, however, was that if he yelled long and hard enough, his parents would eventually give him what he wanted—attention. Once Mr. and Mrs. A. learned to ignore Robby's wailing altogether, the problem disappeared in a few days. What's more, Robby soon started to feel much better about going to bed, as well as about himself in general.

Throwing tantrums, whining, and sulking are probably the most common behaviors that are best dealt with by ignoring. These behaviors, although annoying, never really seem to hurt anyone, and they will usually disappear in short order if systematically ignored. Destructive behaviors, on the other hand, behaviors that pose threats to property and personal safety, are probably best handled with time out.

"Single-occurrence" behaviors are also appropriate for ignoring. By "single-occurrence" we mean those behaviors which occur that you've not seen before. A good example might be the child who, in a fit of anger or frustration, swears for the first time in your presence. If you ignore it, it may never happen again. If you make a big deal out of it, however, your child may simply learn another inappropriate and easy way to get lots of your interest and attention. In this sense, ignoring can be considered a preventative measure. If unacceptable behavior can be ignored when it first appears, the chances are quite good it will disappear just as fast as it appeared. And if it doesn't, you can always turn to mild social disapproval and/or time out.

Speaking of mild social disapproval and time out, ignoring plays a critical part in the proper use of each of these parenting techniques. The effectiveness of both procedures depends heavily on a parent's ability to ignore the child's excess verbiage and excuses. A parent who can't ignore his child's repeated protests, doesn't stand much of a chance of succeeding with either mild social disapproval or time out. Therefore, it really pays to master the art of ignoring.

Consistency:
The *Sine Qua Non* of Ignoring

Consistency is the essence of ignoring. When parents decide to ignore one of their child's behaviors, they are, in effect, making a commitment. That is, they are committing themselves to ignore that particular behavior at almost all costs, and this can be somewhat trying at times. Psychological research data indicate that ignored behaviors often get worse before they get better. Let's suppose, for example, that your child throws a temper tantrum every time he doesn't get his own way. Well, if you start ignoring him when he behaves like that, at first he may simply escalate his tantrums. Eventually he'll realize, however, that throwing tantrums just doesn't pay off anymore, and once he does, the tantrums will begin to occur less frequently. We're only telling you this so that you won't be surprised when things seem to get worse when you first begin to ignore. So hang in there. The behavior *will* change if you stick with your policy of ignoring. Just knowing that should make it a little easier for you. If tantrums or sulking should turn into destructive behaviors, however, you'll probably want to change your approach and start using time out.

Ignoring can also be especially difficult to use in public places or at social gatherings. When a child starts screaming in the supermarket, it can be very embarrassing, indeed, for his parents. Here again, ignoring demands commitment. You simply have to stick to your plan if ignoring is going to work. You can avoid such unpleasant public scenes altogether, however, by planning your schedule so that the tantrum-prone child simply doesn't get the opportunity to embarrass you publicly. You might leave him at home, for example, until his tantrum behavior has been substantially reduced. Of course, this assumes that you have babysitters available and the money to pay for them. At any rate, if you don't feel that you can tolerate the "behavior-to-be-ignored" long enough for it to disappear on its own, perhaps time out or mild social disapproval would be more appropriate alternatives for you to use.

The Basic Components of Ignoring

Expert use of ignoring is the key to its effectiveness. As such, it is important for parents to learn and master these five basic checkpoints of ignoring.

1. *Look Away from Your Child*

   The first step in successful ignoring involves looking *away* from your child. In previous chapters we have described how direct eye contact in and of itself can be rewarding to children. In keeping with the philosophy that unacceptable behavior does not deserve to be rewarded, we are asking you here to literally turn your back on the misbehaving child when you ignore.

2. *Move Away from Your Child*

   We also discussed in previous chapters how your physical proximity can be rewarding to a child. Thus, it is crucial that you put some physical distance between you and your child when you are ignoring him. At times this may be next to impossible, but our research data suggest that parents must move at least *three feet away* from a misbehaving child for ignoring to be maximally effective. Many parents simply leave the room, and they report having had great success with that approach. Leaving the room is one sure way for parents to avoid unintentionally paying attention to the misbehavior of their children.

3. *Neutral Facial Expression*

Facial expression also plays an important role in ignoring. It can be rewarding for some children simply to get a rise out of their parents. Therefore, it's essential that your facial expression remain matter-of-fact while you ignore. Wearing a neutral facial expression, i.e., neither smiling nor frowning, is an effective means of thwarting your child's efforts to gain your attention via misbehavior. It may sometimes be difficult for you to conceal your annoyance under an impassive expression, especially in the face of a full-blown temper tantrum. You must keep in mind, however, that if your child detects that his behavior is getting to you, the chances of that tantrum being prolonged are that much increased.

4. *Ignore Your Child's Verbalizations*

In the same vein, it is important that you not respond to any of your child's verbalizations. If you do, you are only giving him encouragement to continue misbehaving. It is all right, though, for you to say something like "I'm going to ignore you whenever you whine" or "I'll only talk to you if you stop yelling and screaming" *at the outset.* In a way, that is like setting a rule. That rule, however, must not be stated more than *once*, because repeating the rule too often will simply provide too much attention to the child when he's misbehaving.

5. *Ignore Immediately*

Finally, the ignoring sequence should begin as soon as you become aware of the misbehavior. Like the other parenting, we recommend that you begin ignoring immediately. The sooner you can cut off the supply of attention that maintains the undesirable behavior, the better the results you will get.

Finally, be sure to give your child lots of attention and praise as soon as he begins to behave more appropriately. We cannot say enough about the importance of this aspect of parenting. Ignoring will teach your child that certain behaviors will not be rewarded with your attention. It is up to you, then, to reward him with a substantial dose of praise whenever he begins to engage in more acceptable alternative behaviors. He'll learn better and faster if you follow through in this way, and then you will both be a lot happier.

We have included a couple of scenes for you to role-play using the ignoring procedure. Again, take the time to practice and master this skill. Be sure to include all components of the role-play format, especially the Critique and Instant Replay portions. Going over these role-play scenes should also give you a better idea of the sorts of situations best handled by ignoring. Role-playing has proven repeatedly to be the most effective way for parents to integrate and master all aspects of these important parenting skills.

We took a case recently which highlighted for us just how important each component of the ignoring technique really is. Mrs. F. had come to the clinic concerned about the tantrums of her four-year-old daughter, Suzy. After spending a session with her to find out how often the behavior occurred and what form it took, we decided that ignoring would probably be the best way to remedy the situation. Thus, we role-played the ignoring procedure with Mrs. F. a number of times, and then sent her off to deal with those tantrums.

A week later, Mrs. F. called us to say that nothing had changed. In fact, it seemed to her that little Suzy was now having tantrums more than ever. Mrs. F. wanted to try a different approach. We were somewhat surprised to hear this, so we decided to make a home visit to see why the new program was failing. It wasn't too long after we arrived that Suzy obliged us with one of her tantrums and we had an opportunity to observe Mrs. F. in action. It quickly became apparent to us what had gone wrong. As soon as the tantrum began, Mrs. F. moved away from Suzy, kept a neutral facial expression, and said absolutely nothing to her. So far so good. The only problem, however, was simply that Mrs. F. *watched* Suzy while she threw her tantrum. That little bit of parental attention was evidently enough to sustain Suzy's tantrum-throwing behavior. Mrs. F. told us that she found it hard to believe such a little thing as looking at her child could affect the success of the program. We received another call from Mrs. F. about a week later, and this time she was happy as a lark. Suzy wasn't having tantrums anymore. In fact, the entire mother-child relationship had improved. So you can see the importance of learning and practicing the proper use of these parenting skills. *All* of the components are important.

Practice *1*

Scott, your constantly complaining and demanding five-year-old, has repeatedly interrupted your dinner preparations with requests that you give him a cookie. Even though you had told him earlier that a cookie before dinner was out of the question, he has continued to pester you. What do you do?

- ☐ look away from child
- ☐ move at least three feet away from child
- ☐ maintain neutral facial expression
- ☐ ignore *all* of child's verbalizations
- ☐ begin ignoring quickly

Practice *2*

You have just finished using mild social disapproval with Joey. He stops misbehaving, looks you squarely in the eye, and says for the first time ever, "Go to hell!" What do you do?

- ☐ look away from child
- ☐ move at least three feet away from child
- ☐ maintain neutral facial expression
- ☐ ignore *all* of child's verbalizations
- ☐ begin ignoring quickly

7 ❧ ❧

Questions and Answers

IN THIS CHAPTER we will respond to a number of questions commonly asked us by parents, both in the clinic and outside. The questions deal with a wide range of special problems in child raising, including how to use parenting skills in various particular problem situations.

Q: My oldest boy is punished with a time out each time I catch him fighting with his brothers. I know that sometimes he doesn't start these fights. Should I send him to time out on those occasions?

A: Yes, if a child really wants to, he can usually avoid a fight. Even if he is being provoked unfairly by his brothers (and it's usually hard to determine that), he still has earned a time out whenever he fights. At the same time, your household rule about fighting should not just mention your oldest boy but rather anyone who is fighting. Fighting always includes at least *two* people.

Don't even try to determine who started it. If the rule says that fighting behavior leads to time out, then be consistent. Every time *anyone* is engaged in fighting, send both parties to time out. Don't get caught in the trap of trying to be a referee.

Q: I've tried time out with my child, but I seem to be getting nowhere with it. He still disobeys me repeatedly. What should I do?

A: Look for ways in which your child may be getting rewarded by the time out procedure. Does your child find anything to *do* in time out? Are you including *all* the skill components? Is the time-out period long enough? Have you set up a *clear* and *enforceable* rule about when time out will be used? If you can answer positively to these questions, perhaps the problem lies in your "follow-through." Increase your rate of praising for more appropriate behaviors, keeping in mind the seven basic checkpoints of effective praising. In other words, pay lots of attention to your boy when he does do as you ask. Make cooperation well worth his while. If none of these aforementioned adjustments seems to make any difference, you may need to institute a more specialized home program. We'll be describing the ins and outs of such programs in the second part of this book.

Q: Is it ever advisable to spank?

A: Not really. Why spank when you have other simpler and more loving techniques available to you? We realize that there will be times when nothing would seem quite as rewarding *to you* as paddling your child's behind, but it's not worth the hassle and hard feelings. Besides, kids will often start to avoid someone who spanks them a lot. You certainly don't want that, nor do you want to teach your child that aggressive behavior (i.e., yours) is constructive and a preferred solution to problems. Try time out, ignoring, or mild social disapproval. Everyone involved will be happier if you do.

Q: Isn't a child supposed to help out and obey his parents? Why should parents have to praise a child for every little thing he does?

A: Effective parenting skills, featuring lots of praise for constructive behavior, are the best teaching aids a parent can use. For a child, learning what his parents expect in the way of good manners, courtesy, and responsibility may be harder than learning geometry. It also may be harder to teach, so don't be discouraged if your child hasn't picked up all the fine points yet. Praise good manners, approximations to courtesy, fulfilling responsibilities, etc., while using mild social disapproval for poor examples of each. If you are consistent in using these procedures, then you are teaching your child values as effectively as possible.

Q: What relevance do the parenting skills have for toilet training my 2½-year-old?

A: We can't go into detail here about how to toilet train your child, but we can say that much of a child's toileting behavior can be shaped by parental attention. Just think, for example, of all the attention a child usually gets when he wets or soils his pants. He'll be scolded, cleaned up, dressed, and so on. Now that is a lot of attention, and he really doesn't have to expend any great effort to get it. Wetting pants is easy to do, especially for 2½-year-olds. To avoid rewarding such inappropriate behavior, parents might do well to pay as little attention as possible to "mistakes." At the same time, it is important to encourage appropriate toileting behavior with lots of praise. Make a big deal out of it each time he succeeds. Also, don't expect total mastery right away. At first, you may have to praise your child just for telling you that he's messed his pants. Now that may not seem very praiseworthy to you, but it's a start. Before long he'll begin to warn you *before* he messes, and that's half the battle. At any rate, use lots of praise to shape your child's behavior, and be sure to notice and praise each small step along the way to "perfect" toileting behavior.

Q: My daughter's teacher told me that my daughter has "a poor self-concept." I'd like to change that, but in the beginning of the book you told me I had to work with specific behaviors. Is "self-concept" a behavior I can work with?

A: No, but you can work with a number of behaviors that contribute to self-concept. Generally speaking, a poor self-concept is developed through negative feedback from others. That is, when enough people have criticized or ignored a child's efforts at positive and constructive behavior, the child soon begins to feel inadequate. She learns, in effect, that what she does is simply not very praiseworthy. Eventually, that child may come to see herself as a virtual nobody. That is what the term "poor self-concept" means.

The way to correct for this lack of self-esteem is rather straightforward. Rule Number One is that parents should minimize using criticism, and other forms of negative feedback to the child. At the same time, an effort should be made to praise the child for even minimal accomplishments. Give her simple tasks to do, thus guaranteeing success. Play easy games with her so she can win now and then. If you praise liberally during these activities, the child will soon start to feel better about herself and what she does. And this should give her the encouragement she needs to accomplish even more in the future, both at home and in school.

Q: My husband and I both work during the day, so we don't have a lot of time to spend with our children. Will these techniques work for us?

A: Definitely. If you don't get as much time as you might like to spend with your kids, you certainly want that time to be *quality* time. The parenting skills presented here are ideally suited for parents who want to make the most out of the time spent with their children. They are easy to learn, easy to use, and they convey the love and concern you have for your children. What's more, you can use these skills anywhere, be it at the zoo, in the store, at grandmother's house, and so on.

One word of caution to working parents is needed here. When people feel that they have just a little time to spend with their kids, they often bend over backwards trying to please them. Well, pleasing children is laudable, but be careful not to spoil your kids. If you do, you may end up liking them less, and that's not healthy. Use effective parenting skills to encourage your children in more constructive behavior. Then both you and your children will enjoy the time you share together a lot more.

Q: My child seems to be very afraid of the dark. He won't go to sleep at night without a light on. I don't know how to use rewards and punishments to change that. What should I do?

A: *Gradually* acclimate him to the dark on a step-by-step basis over an extended period of time. For example, you might purchase a rheostat and install it in his bedroom. Then each night you can reduce the brightness of his light by just a little from that of the previous night. If you proceed in small enough steps, your child will eventually be able to fall asleep in total darkness. Be sure to praise the child heavily each time he masters one of the small steps along the way. It is most important that you avoid being critical of a fearful child. By the same token, however, some firmness and consistency are required. You might even make a game out of the entire process. In that way, it will be more fun for him and you, sort of a cooperative parent-child venture that is rewarding for both.

If the fear of the dark persists, or if other fears develop, it's quite possible that the child is using his fears to elicit parental attention. If that is indeed the case, chances are that ignoring his fearful behavior will work best, while trying to pay more attention to him at other times of the day. Most children develop irrational fears at one time or another. It seems to be part of growing up. For the most part, they seem to disappear as quickly as they appeared. We'll be talking about how to help the fearful child in more detail later on in the book.

Q: What's so special about these techniques? Haven't most of them been around for years?

A: You bet! And they have stayed around for years for one very good reason. They work. True, these parenting skills have been used previously by parents, but they have been used rather haphazardly, for the most part. In this book, we have delineated precisely everything you need to know in order to make them work for you and thus build better relationships in your home. Our approach is based on a great deal of scientific research, and, as such, it has been proven effective. Never before have these skills been tied together for parents into such a coherent and yet flexible package. What's more, the role-play approach to parent training substantially enhances the ease with which these skills can be mastered. Again, the basic techniques are not really new, but years of scientific research have honed and refined them into maximally effective parenting skills.

Q: I don't really have any of the discipline problems you've described, but I do get some backtalk now and then, especially when my child is tired or keyed up. I usually just ignore him when he acts like that. Am I doing the right thing?

A: That depends. If talking back just recently became part of your child's repertoire, ignoring is probably the most prudent procedure to use. Cutting off *all* your attention to him whenever he behaves like this should let him know that talking back simply doesn't pay off. If, on the other hand, your child has been talking back to you for some time now, you had better tackle the problem straight on before it becomes a more persistent (and annoying) habit. Mild social disapproval has always worked well in situations like this, since it gets your point across firmly with only a minimum of your attention. Of course, if your child continues to backtalk, then you'll probably need to set a rule and enforce it with time out.

Q: I would love to reward my daughter for dressing herself, but the problem is that she never does it. How can I praise a behavior that never occurs?

A: You can't, but there is a remedy to your situation. In such cases parents need to *shape* their children's behavior gradually. Start small and then work up toward bigger things. To encourage a child to dress herself, for example, many parents have had great success by making a game out of it. They might have the child put on her shoes, and then the parent will tie them. In the same way, having a child put a shirt on halfway before the parent puts the other arm through or buttons it gets the child into the act. Gradually, the number of steps required by the child can be increased, while at the same time parental involvement can be decreased. Lots of praise is needed at each and every step of the way. That insures optimum learning, as well as keeping the "dressing game" a positive experience for the child. One word of warning: Don't expect too much too soon. Avoid criticism or any other displays of impatience. Remember, it's a lot easier for your child to let you dress her. You are encouraging her to do this herself, and it is up to you to make sure that this new behavior is rewarding enough for her to want to continue with it.

Q: My two boys are somewhat of a problem at bedtime. They usually talk and giggle in bed for an hour or so, and at times they'll even get out of bed, turn on the light, and start playing with their toys. I've tried scolding, and even spanking them, but nothing seems to work. What do you think I should do?

A: If all they're doing is talking and giggling, you probably shouldn't worry about it. They'll fall asleep when they're tired. Maybe their bedtime is a little early. You might thus experiment with changing the time they go to bed. When children get out of bed to play, however, it's time for you to be more assertive. Mild social disapproval might be useful here. Time out and ignoring, on the other hand, are usually not very effective with bedtime behaviors. When you think about it, bedtime is a sort of a natural time out for kids, so the threat of a time out is really rather weak. Also, ignoring won't get you anywhere since your boys seem to be rewarding each other with lots of attention. So all in all, mild social disapproval is probably the best technique to use for this kind of problem. Be sure to let the kids know you mean business. You can even beef up this new approach with a new rule. Turning on the light and playing after bedtime, for example, might be punished by a bedtime fifteen minutes earlier on the following night. If you follow through on this, they'll soon find out that goofing off at bedtime is no longer worth it.

We'd like to give you two additional tips for dealing with bedtime problems. First, always get the children up at the same time every morning. Don't let them sleep late. If you do, they will be more likely to resist going to bed that night. Second, taper off evening activities as bedtime approaches. Rough-and-tumble play right before bed can leave kids keyed up and make it hard for them to sleep. Finally, be sure to praise children when they exhibit cooperative bedtime behavior. Of course, you don't want to wake them up to praise them, so make a big deal out of it the next morning.

Q: My three-year-old daughter won't share. What can I do about it?

A: Since three-year-olds have only rarely been known to praise each other for sharing, it's usually up to a parent or nursery-school teacher to show a youngster that sharing can be a rewarding experience. Sharing must be taught. Perhaps the best way for you, as a parent, to teach your child sharing is to prompt her whenever she is in a "sharing situation." You might say something like, "It would be *so* nice of you to share those crayons with Nancy." This kind of a prompt signals the child what kind of behavior you see as desirable. If she doesn't share after this prompt, try another. Above all, however, don't criticize or punish her. Remember, you want to demonstrate how *pleasant* sharing can be. At any rate, when she finally does decide to share those crayons, shower her with your attention and praise. If you do, she'll be more likely to share her things again in the future. For older children who have already learned to share, however, you don't have to be quite so patient. They know that sharing is expected of children, and usually a quick reminder or mild social disapproval is enough to get them back on the right track if they "forget."

Q: What about tantrums in stores? I'm still confused about how to deal with my five-year-old when he "starts off" in the market.

A: Tantrums in public places are hard to ignore, unless you're wearing earmuffs and a blindfold. Your best bet usually is to use mild social disapproval to try to nip the tantrum in the bud. If that fails, you'll probably have to impose a make-shift time out. Lead the child out of the store and put him in the car for several minutes. You should remain in the driver's seat during this time (remember, it's fun for kids to pretend they're driving a car) and try to totally ignore him. Once he's been quiet for several minutes, you can take him back in the store and finish your shopping. If he decides to throw another tantrum, you'll simply have to repeat the procedure. As you read this, you may be thinking something like, "What a pain! I can't stop whatever I'm doing every five minutes just to discipline a screaming kid." If you can't, you're probably better off leaving him home in the first place. If that's not possible, you're just going to have to stick with the time out. If you have set up a rule about tantrums beforehand, however, and back up that rule with action, you'll probably get the desired behavior changes after one or two instances of time out.

Q: I've got a little boy who eats like a bird. He's skinny as a rail, but he always insists that he's not hungry. Should I make him eat more?

A: Don't "make him" eat more; encourage him instead. Give him lots of praise for eating even minimal amounts at first. Eating will soon become a more pleasant and rewarding activity for him.

Actually, poor appetites are quite common among youngsters. Usually, a child doesn't want to eat for one of two reasons. Either he'd rather be doing something else at that moment, such as watching a good TV show or playing with friends, or else he doesn't eat because that's a guaranteed way to get some attention from you. In either case, parents have reported having a good deal of success by setting rules. One good rule is "you don't have to eat it, but you have to sit here with us until dinner is over." Once you've said that you can then ignore any subsequent excuses and protests. Be sure to keep an eye on his eating, though, because if he then starts to take a couple mouthfuls, you've got to reward him quickly and enthusiastically with some praise and attention.

Q: I always thought it was important to reason with a child and explain to him in detail why you are unhappy with his behavior.

A: Repeated attempts to reason with a child teach him one thing for sure—that misbehavior on his part will reap lots of your attention. It may also teach him that, if he's clever enough, there's a good chance he can talk his way out of punishment. Most children know when they're misbehaving. Just a few words, direct and easy to understand, are all that's usually required to encourage them to behave more constructively.

Q: I've been told that many forms of misbehavior are simply ways for the child to express himself. I've also been told that a child who is allowed to express himself freely is better adjusted. What about that?

A: Children certainly should be permitted to express themselves. No one can argue with that. Some means of self-expression are more desirable than others, however, and it is up to you to encourage your child to use these more appropriate ways.

It has become popular in recent years, both in school settings and child-guidance clinics, to encourage both parents and teachers to give children more freedom. Of course, this is good advice for those individuals who keep too tight a rein on their kids. Nobody likes a dictator. For the most part, however, we feel that youngsters need some limits set for them. Research shows that setting limits consistently and stating expectations serve to make children feel more secure, and in that sense, better adjusted. It just makes sense that a child would feel more confident and secure knowing exactly what you expect of him. It is often difficult for young children to handle too much freedom, and most welcome some sort of parental guidance and instruction. We recommend our parenting skills to you as the simplest, most effective, and most human techniques available for teaching your children exactly what you expect from their behavior. If you use them well, we can almost guarantee you a better adjusted child and more harmonious family interactions.

Q: My kids don't cause me any problem. Should I bother learning these parenting skills?

A: That's up to you. Actually, you may be using some of these skills right now and just don't realize it. At any rate, if you're having success with your present style of parenting, we certainly wouldn't want you to change anything. You may want to keep this book in your library, however, in case unexpected behavior problems should arise. Keep up the good work.

SECTION 2
Special Situations and Specialized Procedures

8 ◅§ ৡ▻

Special Incentive Programs

So FAR we have acquainted you with a set of flexible parenting skills which allow parents to build better family relationships through the systematic distribution of their attention. We know of no other approaches to child raising which can offer you as much in terms of effectiveness. In our clinic work, however, we occasionally encounter a child who presents a special problem for his parents. His behavior is no longer responsive to social rewards and punishments. Perhaps he has been behaving in certain ways for so long that it is unusually hard for him to change. Perhaps misbehavior is so rewarding to him that in comparison parental attention is simply not powerful enough to make him want to change. Perhaps he has been virtually ignored and neglected by his parents for quite some time now, and, as a result, the power of parental attention to encourage more appropriate behavior has dwindled. Whatever the reason, one thing is clear.

Parents in a situation like this must look for more powerful ways to reward their child for behaving appropriately. Of course, these rewards have to be more desirable than those maintaining the undesirable behaviors. There is a great deal of scientific research to show that the special incentive program is uniquely effective in supplying the supplemental reward power required to generate constructive behavior change in these children.

The Special Incentive Program: What Is It?

Special incentive programs are noted for their ability to motivate children for positive behavior change right away. Under such a program, a child can earn points (or stars, poker chips, etc.) for behaving in certain ways. These points are not rewards in and of themselves, of course, but they can later be "cashed in" by the child for various tangible rewards and/or special privileges. The concept is elementary. Special incentive programs are based on those very same principles of behavior change which we outlined for you in Chapter Two and from which effective parenting skills have been derived. If a child behaves appropriately, he is then rewarded. If he doesn't, he gets no reward. It's as simple as that. As a general rule, though, special incentive programs are more formalized, more expensive, less flexible, and less personal than the parenting skills we presented in Section I. For that reason we heartily recommend that parents try praise, mild social disapproval, time out, and ignoring *before* implementing a special incentive program.

We recognize that special incentive programs are not

as easy to use as some might think, so here is a step-by-step description of how to design and operate one of these programs.

The Anatomy of a Special Incentive Program

There are eight basic ingredients essential to the success of any home incentive program. What follows is a detailed explanation of each. Read carefully, because failure to understand or carry out even one of these procedures can spell disaster for your program.

1. *Behavior Definition*

Before you can even begin to think about anything else, you must *define the behavior* you plan to change. This means that you'll probably need to spend some time closely observing your child's behavior. See if you can determine *exactly* what he's doing or not doing that upsets you. Be as specific as possible. Vague definitions, such as "being selfish" or "acting like a baby" just won't suffice. Be sure you specify *behaviors*. For example, "being selfish" might be translated into "not sharing toys with other children." In the same way, "acting like a baby" might be better defined as "whining," "following mother around the house," or "baby-talk." The point is that children engage in certain *behaviors* which make them seem "selfish" or "babyish," and so on. It is your job, as supervisor of the home incentive program, to determine exactly what those behaviors are.

Strict behavioral definition is important from

yet another standpoint. Home incentive programs are based on the notion that positive behavior deserves to be rewarded. Parents who can specify *in detail* what they consider to be positive behavior will avoid a lot of confusion when it comes time to determine whether the behavior of their children does, in fact, merit reward. So, take a little time at the outset to define the situation in clear, behavioral terms. Program success often hinges upon not having to haggle with your child about program requirements.

2. *Count the Behavior*

Once you have defined the behaviors you'd like to see changed, it is essential that you determine just how often those behaviors occur. This is important for two reasons. First, it gives you a better idea of the seriousness of the situation. It may seem as if a child is *constantly* fighting, for example, yet when his parents begin counting fights they are often surprised to see that the situation is really not as bad as they had previously imagined. Second, keeping a daily count of the behaviors will later provide a handy reference for comparison. That is, you can compare how often the behavior occurred before and after starting the home program. In this way, it will be easier for you to determine whether or not your home program is working. Keep a daily tally of the target behavior(s) for at least *one week* prior to implementing the special incentive program. In our experience we have found that many parents are so anxious to get started on their home programs that they often neglect this very important preliminary step. Later on they realize, however, that they have no way of assessing the effectiveness of their program. Don't skip over this important step. It's essential to program success.

3. *The Reward Menu*

This third step involves a joint parent-child cooperative effort. Sit down with your child and find out just what things are rewarding to him. Spend some time during this stage to list carefully a number of items or activities that your child will want to strive for. These will be the rewards your child can choose from when he has behaved constructively. To help you with this, we've included here a list of questions you can ask your child. These will help him to think about exactly what's rewarding for him.

REWARD QUESTIONS

- What do you like to do for fun?
- What kind of presents do you like?
- What hobbies do you have?
- What would you buy if you had 50¢, $1, or even $5?
- What would you hate to lose?
- Where do you like to go for fun?
- What sorts of things do you like to have? Clothes? Toys? Books?
- What sorts of things do you do a lot of the time? Watch TV? Read? Play baseball? Color?

Honest answers to the above questions should provide you with enough material to form a varied and appealing *menu of rewards*. Be sure to have a wide enough assortment of rewards so that your child won't get bored with the home program. Variety is the spice of life when it comes to reward menus. For example, provide some rewards that he can buy on a day-to-day basis, as well as other, larger rewards that he can "save" for. In this way, you will give him a choice as to when and how he wants to spend his points. Your child will be more motivated just knowing that his reward menu has a number of goodies and fun activities for him to choose from.

Before we leave our discussion of the reward menu, however, there are several key issues which must be considered. The first is *expense*. If you're not careful, a special incentive program can cost you a lot of money. If you're rewarding good behavior with new toys, candy, books, etc., you're going to run up some bills. For this reason, we recommend that your reward menu include mostly inexpensive activities and special privileges. An extra hour of TV time and being allowed to go fishing with friends are two good examples of such inexpensive yet rewarding activities. If possible, try to include a number of activities which involve other family members. If your child earns enough points, for example, he might "buy" the family a trip to the zoo, to a baseball game, or even to the local ice-cream parlor. In addition to bringing family members closer together, such activities provide opportunities for parents, brothers, and sisters to praise the child not only for behaving so well but also for generously "buying" a treat for the whole family with his points.

A second consideration to keep in mind when compiling a reward menu is *access*. If a child *already* has access to certain rewards, he probably won't be very motivated to change his behavior in order to obtain them. Try to think of *new* and *different* rewards, privileges he doesn't have now but would like to have in the future. In short, if your child is already getting just about everything he wants, it may be difficult to come up with a list of new and desirable rewards. If that is the case, have him start earning some of those rewards he has already been getting. Try to choose *special* privileges and activities for the reward menu. If your child already gets to stay up at night as late as he wants, he probably won't be very enthused about spending his points for the privilege of staying up a half hour later. Why should he buy what he's already getting free of charge? Make behavior change a worthwhile goal for your child by making sure you have control over his access to those rewards.

Finally, reward menus need to be *reviewed and adjusted* now and then. Everyone gets tired of the same old thing; children are no exception. Try to think of new and creative activities which you can periodically add to the menu to whet the youngster's appetite. It will keep him interested, and that's essential to maintaining behavior changes. Be sure to check with your child, however, before adding new rewards. Remember, what may seem rewarding to you may not interest him in the least.

4. *The Exchange Ratio*

Once you have pinpointed the target behaviors and drawn up an appealing reward menu, it is time to figure out the exchange ratios. That is, you need to determine (1) how many points the

child can earn by behaving appropriately, and
(2) how many points it takes to "buy" the various
items and privileges on the reward menu. Sim-
plicity is the cardinal rule to keep in mind when
figuring out the *exchange ratios*. If you make
things too complicated, everyone will wind up
confused and possibly even unhappy. Later on in
this chapter we will present a sample special incentive program from our case files. That example
should provide you with some ideas about how
to structure your point system. For now, however,
let's look at some general guidelines which parents must follow in determining a fair and equitable exchange ratio.

First of all, you don't want the home program
to be *too difficult* for your child. That is, you
want him to be able to earn enough points so
that he can "purchase" rewards when he's behaved
appropriately. On the other hand, if the program
is *too easy* for your child, he'll be able to buy
those rewards without having to work at changing
his behavior very much. Your job, then, is to find
the middle ground, where the child must show
some changes to earn points, but it's not so difficult that he rarely earns enough points to purchase a reward.

The first step involves setting reasonable expectations on the child's behavior. If you plan on
sudden or major behavior changes right away,
you are probably going to be disappointed. Behavior doesn't change overnight. This is usually
a gradual process. Therefore, you'll want to set
up your home program so that *gradual* changes
get rewarded. This is where counting the target

behavior comes in handy. Refer back to your daily tallies of how often the target behavior occurred. If the average number of tantrums per day was five, for example, you might want to award one point for days with only four tantrums, two points for days with three tantrums, etc. In this way, the child is rewarded for showing any kind of improvement, and the rewards are increased as the improvement increases. You might even want to include a *bonus point* or two for perfect performances, i.e., tantrum-free days.

The second step consists of setting prices on the rewards. If the child behaves perfectly, he should have enough points to "buy" a substantial reward. On the other hand, if he shows just a little behavior improvement, then he should only be able to purchase one of the smaller rewards. Continuing with our tantrum example, let's say that this particular child has earned six points for going a whole day without tantrums (five points for no tantrums plus one bonus point for a perfect day). He should then be able to buy one of the "bigger" rewards on the menu, such as going to McDonald's for a hamburger (worth six points), or two or three of the "smaller" rewards, such as a candy bar (two points) and an extra hour of TV time (four points). As you can see, the best thing about a program like this is that the child gets to choose exactly how he wants to spend the points he's earned. The most important thing to remember, however, is that the program should reward even small improvements. This must be a *positive* experience for the child if the program is to work. Don't be surprised if you have to fiddle with the point system and reward prices for a while, however, before hitting upon the most effective balance. It is far better for parents to make necessary adjustments than to stick with exchange ratios that sabotage the effectiveness of your program.

5. *Charting*

Kids love charts. Charts let children know how well they are doing. They provide visible evidence of good work on their part. A chart showing lots of improvement and successes is something almost any child can be proud of. Therefore, it's important that you post an *attractive* chart in some prominent place in your home. We have found refrigerator doors to be exceptionally fine locations for program charts. It's also helpful to post the reward menu close by, including the price of each reward. Here's a sample chart and reward menu for the child in our tantrum example.

Sun.	Mon.	Tues.	Wed.	Thurs.	Fri.	Sat.
2	1	2	2	1	0	3
3	2	3	4	6	4	6
6	6	6	6			

4 tantrums = 1 point
3 tantrums = 2 points
2 tantrums = 3 points
1 tantrum = 4 points
0 tantrums = 6 points

Reward Menu	
Candy Bar	1
½ hr. TV	2
Bedtime Story	3
McDonald's	6
Play Cards with Parents	4
Ice Cream	2
New Story Book	15
New Football	30
Fishing Trip (1 day)	36
Trip to the Zoo	30
Play outside for 1 hr. extra	2

Notice how this child has the choice of spending his points for a small reward each day, or else saving them up to buy larger rewards later. We will be showing you another chart and reward menu later on in this chapter.

6. *Praise*

In light of the fact that a home program should be a positive experience, it is important that you praise your child liberally every time he earns a point or buys a reward. Be sure to use all of the seven praise components. You certainly don't want to be using a special incentive program forever. Your goal as a parent should be to establish the rewarding qualities of your praise and attention as quickly as possible. Once that is accomplished, then social rewards and punishments will be more than sufficient to promote positive behavior changes.

By the same token, avoid criticizing when your

child fails to earn points and rewards. If he doesn't earn a reward, that is his choice. His penalty is simply not being rewarded. Don't compound that penalty with criticism, or he may grow to dislike you and the home program. Of course, once that happens, everyone is a loser.

Almost as important as avoiding criticism is avoiding lengthy haggling about how many points your child's behavior has earned. As we pointed out in Step 1, clear and specific behavior definitions will prevent a lot of confusion later on. If you have defined your expectations clearly, however, and there is still some disagreement, just remember one thing. *You* are the boss. *You* are handing out the rewards, so *you* have the last word. Of course, you have to be fair and give rewards when the child's behavior has earned them, but you don't have to argue with him nonproductively. Your best bet is simply to restate the behavior desired and the number of points he's earned that day. Don't reward angry outbursts, protests, and excuses with your attention. If you're consistent with this, as well as lavish with your praise for appropriate behavior, you really shouldn't have any hassles over program fairness. If your youngster complains about not having enough points to stay up past bedtime, for example, you need only remind him that it was his choice not to earn more points that day. You can then rest your case.

7. *Adjustments*

If you're keeping up with the daily charting, you should have a pretty good idea of how the home program is working. If your child has shown gradual and consistent improvement, the program is accomplishing exactly what it was designed to do. If, after a week or two, however, you can see that the program is not working, then you will probably need to make some adjustments. Above all, don't panic and scrap the entire program. Special incentive programs are somewhat complex, and as such, it is a common occurrence for parents to have to make one or more program adjustments before hitting on the "right" formula. Go back and review each of the procedures we have outlined for you so far.

8. *Phasing Out the Program*

Once you are satisfied with your child's behavior, it is time for you to begin thinking about gradually phasing out the home program. The first and most important aspect of this procedure simply involves stepping up the amount of praising you do. This serves to make praise as powerful a reward for your child as almost any item on the reward menu.

There are several acceptable alternatives for parents to choose from when considering how best to phase out the home incentive program. The first simply involves gradually setting higher behavioral standards for earning the same number of points, while at the same time adding new items to the reward menu. Make certain, however, that these new rewards are appealing to the child. Otherwise, this approach may backfire.

A second alternative might be to sit down with your child and negotiate a time limit on the program. Then, at the end of the mutually agreed-upon time period, both parents and child can reevaluate the program and decide whether or not it needs to be continued. Be sure to include your child in this process. Arbitrary decisions made by parents are often resisted, and justifiably so, by children in these situations.

A third option would be to reduce *gradually* the number of hours each day that the incentive program is in effect. As the child begins to respond to praise given frequently and lavishly during "open time"—i.e., time when the program is not in effect—he will need fewer and fewer points and tangible rewards. In this way, the home incentive program can be gradually diminished to the vanishing point.

After several weeks of this gradual program fading with continued good behavior, you will probably be ready to close out the program altogether. A good way to do this is to have a small "graduation" party or some other special and significant event. Make the child feel as if he's really accomplished something, *because he has.* Once the program has been discontinued, you can then begin encouraging positive behavior via social rewards and punishments. Remember, the program allowed your child to receive handsome rewards for behaving appropriately. Now more than ever you need to praise him for every example of good behavior. If you fail to follow through in this fashion, you may very well undo all of the good things accomplished by the home program.

One word of caution is in order here. Once the program has been discontinued, your child may slip up now and then. Don't be alarmed, no child is perfect. They all misbehave occasionally. Infrequent "slip-ups" are not indicators that your special program failed. Use mild social disapproval to deal with them. If the "slip-ups" begin to occur at a rate comparable to that before you started the special program, however, you should think seriously about reinstating it. Home programs are designed to teach children new and more constructive ways of behaving. Perhaps you ended the program before the new behaviors became solid habits. If the old program was effective, bring it out of retirement and use it again. It's not a sign of failure. It's simply a sign that you didn't stick with it long enough. So go ahead and try it again. You've got nothing to lose and everything to gain.

A Pause to Review

Let's take a few moments here to summarize the material we've covered so far. Special incentive programs are most successful when parents keep in mind the eight basic ingredients. These ingredients are:

1. Problem definition in behavioral terms
2. Counting the target behavior(s)
3. The reward menu
4. The exchange ratios
5. Charting
6. Praise for positive behavior changes
7. Program adjustments
8. Phasing out the program

Now we will show you step by step how one pair of beleaguered parents solved their problems via a special incentive program. This is an actual case example taken from our clinic experience. The program used proved to be highly effective in changing several persistent and annoying child behaviors.

The Case of Alan M.: From Slob to Saint in Seven Weeks

Mr. and Mrs. M. had been working with us for several weeks around the issue of their son's sloppiness. Their only child, Alan, was eight years old, and for as long as Mr. and Mrs. M. could remember, he simply refused to pick up after himself. Not only was his room always an absolute mess, but he repeatedly cluttered the living room, den, and kitchen with his toys, books, and other paraphernalia. His parents had tried all kinds of approaches, but nothing seemed to make any difference. From our first-hand observations of the M. household, it quickly became apparent to us that Alan had indeed developed some very bad habits which were probably going to be quite resistant to change. He was not very responsive to social rewards and punishments, so we decided on a special incentive program as the wisest course of action. What follows is a play-by-play description of how Mr. and Mrs. M. put together and carried out their home program.

1. Problem Definition

After closely observing Alan's behavior for several days, Mr. and Mrs. M. came up with the following list of behaviors they would like to see from their son more often.

1. Putting clothes away in the closet and dresser
2. Putting toys away in the toy chest
3. Putting books away in the bookcase
4. Making the bed

2. *Counting the Behaviors*

We liked the looks of Mr. and Mrs. M.'s behavior list. The behaviors were clearly defined and, as such, easily counted. We next instructed them to count how often these behaviors occurred. To do this, we had them make three spot checks of their house each day, one at 8:00 A.M., one at 5:00 P.M., and the other at 8:00 P.M. They used a daily tally sheet which looked like this:

BEHAVIORS	8 A.M.	5 P.M.	8 P.M.
1. CLOTHES PUT AWAY			
2. TOYS PUT AWAY			
3. BOOKS PUT AWAY			
4. BED MADE			
DATE _____			

If all of Alan's clothes were put away at 8 A.M., for example, Mr. and Mrs. M. simply put a check mark in the appropriate box, as shown above. After observing and recording their son's behavior in this fashion for seven days, they developed a pretty good idea of just how sloppy Alan really was. During that period, he made his bed once, but at no time were his clothes, toys, or books put away. Thus, it turned out that Alan really was as messy as they had previously thought.

3. *The Reward Menu*

Next, Mr. and Mrs. M. sat down with Alan one night after supper to draw up a varied and appealing reward menu. Here's what they all came up with:

```
REWARD MENU

Cherry pie for dessert
Model airplane (less than $2)
New book
"G.I. Joe" toy
Trip to the local aquarium
Trip to the local zoo
High-school football game
Staying up half hour later at night
"Pop Tarts" for breakfast
Helping Dad in his workshop
Playing outside after school
Playing Monopoly with Mom and Dad
Playing Ping-Pong with Dad
New baseball mitt
Puppy
Trip to local amusement park
```

You can see that Mr. and Mrs. M. included a wide assortment of reward items, family activities, and special privileges. Also, some rewards were big; some were little. The most important thing about his reward menu, however, was that it got Alan pretty excited at the prospect of earning some of these rewards.

4. *The Exchange Ratios*

Once the reward menu had been put together, the M. family members put their heads together to come up with a point system and some fair reward prices. As it turned out, they decided to continue making those three spot checks each day at 8:00, 5:00, and 8:00, using the same daily tally sheets. Alan now could earn one point for each check mark he received. Thus it was possible for him to earn up to twelve points each day. It was then up to Alan whether or not he wanted to spend his points each day for one or more of the smaller rewards or save them up to "buy" a bigger reward later on. Together with Alan, Mr. and Mrs. M. set the prices for each reward on the menu. The menu now looked like this:

REWARD MENU	
	pts.
Cherry pie for dessert	10
Model Airplane (less than $2)	10
New book	10
"G.I. Joe" toy	12
Trip to local aquarium	20
Trip to local zoo	20
High-school football game	20
Staying up half hour later at night	3
"Pop Tarts" for breakfast	2
Helping Dad in his workshop	4
Playing outside after school	2
Playing Monopoly with Mom and Dad ..	3
Playing Ping-Pong with Dad	2
New baseball mitt	70
Puppy	70
Trip to the local amusement park	20

Once the point system had been worked out, along with the reward prices, the program was ready to get underway. The program rules were then clearly explained once more to Alan, along with the notion that it was now up to him whether or not he earned any of the items on the reward menu.

5. *Charting*

Mr. and Mrs. M. clearly explained the new home program to Alan and then posted a chart on their refrigerator door, along with the reward menu. After the 8:00 P.M. check each day they entered the total number of points Alan had earned that day. They also kept a running total of how many points he saved and how many he had spent. Their chart looked like this:

Behavior	S	M	T	W	T	F	S
1. Clothes Put Away							
2. Toys Put Away							
3. Books Put Away							
4. Bed Made							
Total Pts.							
Pts. Spent							
Total Pts. Saved							

By charting this way, anyone could tell at a glance just how well the program was working for each of the behaviors in question. In addition, it was easy for Alan to keep track of how many points he had to spend on the various items on the menu. Each week Mr. and Mrs. M. posted a new chart on the refrigerator door, making sure to save the old ones for their records.

6. Praising for Appropriate Behavior

Mr. and Mrs. M. had been warned by us not to criticize Alan for failures to earn points. Instead, they were encouraged to praise him enthusiastically each time he earned some points, as well as when he purchased a reward from the menu. We role-played several "praise" sequences with them in order to make sure that they were praising in the most effective fashion.

7. Program Adjustments

Like most home incentive programs, this one began to show some remarkable changes in Alan's behavior. In less than two weeks, he was consistently earning between three and seven points each day. After a couple of weeks more, however, it became apparent to Mr. and Mrs. M. that Alan's behavior was no longer improving. We reviewed their charts, the daily tally sheets, and the reward menu with them in order to figure out why. As a result of this evaluation, we suggested three minor adjustments in the program. First, the reward prices of the smaller rewards were raised an average of four points each. It had simply been too easy for Alan to earn them. Second, we noticed that, although Alan was now regularly putting his books, clothes, and toys away, making his bed was still a problem. Thus, we added a bonus of three points for each "perfect" day. Now it was possible for him to earn fifteen points per day. Finally, we encouraged Mr. and Mrs. M. to double the amount of praising they were presently giving Alan. We also gave them some more coaching on their praise technique. Once these program adjustments were implemented, we are happy to report that Alan quickly began to earn between ten and fifteen points each day. Needless to say, all of the M.'s, Alan included, were quite pleased about the whole thing.

8. Phasing Out the Program

After several weeks of near "perfect" days, Mr. and Mrs. M. began to ask us about phasing out the program. We asked them to be patient, however, because we felt that Alan needed a little more time to solidify his new behavior patterns. After approximately three more weeks of continued behavior improvement, though, we agreed that it was time to begin the program-fading procedures. We raised the reward prices a bit and instructed Mr. and Mrs. M. to inform Alan that he was soon going to "graduate" from the program. Furthermore, if he continued to be so neat around the house, they would continue to take him extra places and do extra fun things with him. Finally, we emphasized to them once more the importance of praise for appropriate behavior. We also trained them in the proper use of mild social disapproval so that they could quickly and effectively deal with occasional "slip-ups." Well, to bring a long story to a close, everything went as planned. The program was successfully withdrawn, and Alan is as neat as anyone can expect of a child his age. He also is quite pleased with himself about this and regards the change process as a positive one.

The moral of this story is that special incentive programs work. Sure, they can be expensive and time consuming, and you may not really like the idea of buying good behavior, but just remember one thing: The whole idea of a special incentive program is to change the behavior of a child who, for one reason or another, no longer responds well to social rewards and punishment.

Thus, as a parent using one of these programs, your goal becomes one of gradually replacing tangible rewards and special privileges with social rewards. Once that happens, your home life will be a lot more enjoyable for you and your children.

9 ⋞ ⋟

Adolescence: Establishing Communication and Trust

LIVING WITH an adolescent is usually nobody's bargain. It generally requires a good deal of patience, tolerance, and understanding. What can you do, for example, when you give your teenager ten dollars to buy himself a new shirt, and he returns with a faded second-hand army jacket instead? What can you say to your daughter when she claims she can't stand any of the clothes in her wardrobe any longer? How about the adolescent who insists there's nothing wrong with smoking "grass" and then has the audacity to criticize his mom and dad for having a drink now and then? Or the seventeen-year-old who lies around the house all day, refusing to do any household chores yet continually griping about having "nothing to do"? Sound familiar? You bet! These are typical everyday problems encountered by parents of teenagers, which, if handled incorrectly, can cause parents to grow old before their time.

The Importance of Peers

Let's take just a moment or two here to find out just why parents often find it so difficult to get along with their adolescent children. Essentially, the problem is one of influence, or rather lack of influence. We have devoted the better part of this book to showing you how children's behavior can be influenced by parental attention. Well, for younger children this is true, but it's just not that simple where teenagers are concerned. Whereas attention from parents is very rewarding to youngsters, adolescents often can take it or leave it. In short, parental attention is no longer a primary influence on adolescent behavior. It's still important; make no mistake about that. Yet there is another source of influence which governs the behavior of these youngsters, and that is the attention of peers.

Think back to the days when you were a teenager. Did you dress to please your parents or to please your friends? Who would you rather have been with on Saturday night —your friends or your parents? Parents may be nice, but they're just not where the action is as far as most adolescents are concerned. Adolescents need to be recognized and accepted by a circle of friends and acquaintances. As such, their behavior is powerfully influenced by the social rewards and punishments of their peers. So don't take it too hard when your teenager informs you that he would rather stay in town with his friends than go on a weekend camping trip with the family. He still loves you. He's just growing up, that's all.

O.K., now that you realize that you're in competition for control of your adolescent's behavior, what can you do to make your relationship with him smoother, more pleasant and more loving? Your adolescent is still a member of the family, and as such, it's only reasonable for you to expect certain things from him in terms of behavior. The question then becomes one of how to make the most out of the influence you do have, while at the same time not "cracking down" so hard that you spoil everyone's fun or generate a "runaway."

To begin with, the parenting skills outlined in Section I of this book are still useful (except time out) in dealing with adolescents. Although they may not work quite as well with adolescent behavior as with the behavior of younger children, praise, mild social disapproval, and ignoring are certainly proven relationship builders for children of all ages. You like to be praised, don't you? Sure you do, and so does an adolescent. Praise is a universal reward. Now think of how often you have praised your teenager lately. If you're like most parents, that's probably not too often. And that's understandable too, given that you probably haven't been all that pleased with his behavior lately. The problem is, however, that a lot of criticism, coupled with insufficient praise, eventually puts a strain on any parent-child relationship. Look at it this way. Would you want to spend a lot of time with someone who rarely lets you know that you're pleasing to him? Of course not. How many divorces, for example, are triggered by the failure of one or both spouses to show and express affection for the other? The point of all this is that you can alienate your adolescent, not only by being too critical but also by failing to praise him when he's earned it.

Mild social disapproval and ignoring, on the other hand, are also quite useful. Both of these techniques enable you to get your message of displeasure across, without having to go into long harangues or lengthy and nonproductive discussions. These techniques are low-key and matter-of-fact. As such, they help keep tempers from flaring on both sides, and when you're dealing with an adolescent, that can be very important.

The Communication Gap

Thus far we have sympathized with the parents of adolescents. Let's not forget, however, that adolescence is usually no picnic for the youngsters, either. They've got problems of their own to worry about. For the first time in their lives, for example, they are faced with taking a stand on such issues as drugs, sex, religion, and politics. Major physical changes are also taking place, and this can be a source of concern and confusion for many youngsters. In addition, they are constantly concerned about their own social skills and their abilities to make and keep friends. The biggest problem for adolescents, however, is that they have to walk that very thin line between pleasing parents and pleasing peers, which is often a case of being damned if you do and damned if you don't. Suffice it to say that adolescence is a time of new experiences and, not infrequently, new problems as well.

So now what have we got? On the one hand, we've got concerned and loving parents who can see their influence gradually slipping away, and on the other, we've got their adolescent children, old enough to start feeling their oats but too young to be allowed to do whatever they feel like doing. Given a situation like this, it is imperative that the lines of communication remain open between all parties concerned. Unfortunately, however, that is often not the case.

Communication between parents and adolescents is many times very punishing to both, and we all know what happens to punished behaviors. They simply aren't very likely to occur again in the future. Such was the case of sixteen-year-old Donald W. and his parents. Here's a portion of the transcript of our initial meeting with them.

> Mrs. W.: So you see, we really want to get along with Donald, but he just doesn't listen to us.
>
> Mr. W.: I'll say! He thinks he knows it all. We can't tell him a thing. (To Donald:) A big know-it-all; that's what you are.
>
> Donald: Well, if you weren't such a goddamned dictator . . .
>
> Mrs. W.: Donald! Don't swear at your father. And he's not a dictator.
>
> Donald: The hell he isn't! He's always on my back about something.
>
> Mr. W.: Listen here, young man! I'll get off your back when you start treating your mother and me with some respect.
>
> Donald: I'll bet! (All three then begin to stare silently ahead, obviously angry.)
>
> Mrs. W.: (To us) You see what happens? This happens every time.
>
> Us: Well, let's take a look at just *how* you people are communicating with one another.

The W. family was obviously suffering from a breakdown in communications. A closer examination of their brief "conversation" revealed the sources of the problem to us. Essentially, Mr. W. and his son disliked not only the things they heard from each other, but they also disliked the way those things were said. Thus, conversation between the two became a source of frustration for each, and tempers usually flared shortly thereafter. What could they have done differently? Well, for starters, they might have observed our four rules for more effective communication.

1. Be a Good Listener

Rule Number One is that you must be a *good listener*. That may sound easy enough, but you'd be surprised at how often people really don't pay any attention to what the other person is trying to say. Being a good listener is more than simply not interrupting the speaker. It's also more than just hearing the words of the speaker. It's hearing *and* trying to understand. People often find it difficult to put into words *exactly* what they're trying to say. No two people think and speak in *exactly* the same terms or phrases. Because of this, the speaker may intend to convey one message, but the listener hears an altogether different message. This occurs frequently when parents and adolescents get together. They simply don't speak the same language. The best way to overcome this obstacle, however, is a procedure called "checking out." When your teenager says something to you, for example, repeat his message back to him *in your own words* and ask him if that's what he meant. In short, "check out" with him whether or not you fully understand what he's just said. This procedure takes very little time or effort, but it prevents a lot of misunderstandings and hard feelings. Of course, being a good listener in no way guarantees that you're going to like what you hear, but at least you'll know for sure what the speaker intends. Phrases like "If I understand you correctly, you mean _____," and "Is this what you are trying to say?" are valuable skills in a parent's repertoire.

2. *Don't Blame; Admit Your Own Feelings*

The second rule of effective communication involves *admitting your feelings* rather than *blaming others*. When Mr. W. said Donald was a "know-it-all" he was, in effect, blaming Donald for the family friction. The initial response of someone who has been blamed is usually to defend himself, or even lash out and blame his accuser for something. This is precisely what Donald did when he responded by calling his dad a "dictator." When blaming starts, nobody wins. People who are too busy defending themselves can rarely work cooperatively to solve problems.

A person who owns up to his feelings, on the other hand, is merely stating a fact. He's not blaming anyone. It even sounds more conciliatory to say, "When _____ happens, I feel _____." Mr. W., for example, might have said, "When I talk with you, it *feels* as if you're not listening to me," or "I get upset when I feel I'm being ignored." Donald, on the other hand, could have said something like, "No matter what I do, I *feel* as if you're not satisfied with me." If both had admitted their feelings in this fashion, their conversation would have been a bit more reasonable and productive.

3. *Deal with Specific Behaviors and Not Character Traits*

When people disagree, they occasionally resort to name-calling and other kinds of derogatory remarks. This sort of communication is probably the least useful one can have, for it not only focuses attention away from the specific issues at hand, but also fans the flames of discord. Rule number three simply asks that you *deal with the specific behaviors* and not the traits or characteristics of the other person. Remember back in Chapter Three where we asked parents to praise behavior and not the child? The same goes for criticism. Mr. W. probably had a legitimate gripe about his son's behavior. To him, it felt as if he wasn't being listened to. Yet Mr. W. didn't confine his criticism to Donald's listening behavior. He criticized his son's personality by calling him a "know-it-all." Similarly, Donald didn't play fair when he labeled his dad a "dictator." The issue at hand was really no more than Donald's wanting his father to "let up" on him a bit. Of course, once the name-calling began, each became more interested in hurting the other than in resolving their differences. So, if your teenager does something you don't like or approve of, don't attack his personality. Try to deal with the issue instead. Even though you'd like to see some behavior change, you still need to let the youngster know that you love and respect him.

4. *Praise Efforts at Communication*

Finally, people need to reward each other for the act of communicating. This is an especially important message for the parents of adolescents to understand. Let your child know that you're glad that he comes to you with his problems. Let him know how much you appreciate talking things over with him. In short, reward your adolescent for communicating with you. Too often parents give the impression that it's just a bother, chore, or source of irritation. It's far better to know what's going on than to have your child shut you out when it comes to talking about important things. Remember, you're in competition with the teenager's peers. They are almost always glad to hear whatever he has to say, and that's pretty rewarding. Make sure you do some rewarding of your own.

Communication Skills: A Review

There are four simple rules for more effective communication. Here they are again, in simplified form.

Four Rules of Effective Communication

1. Be a good listener; *check* to see that you understand
2. Admit your feelings; don't blame
3. Deal with specific behaviors; not personalities
4. Praise your child for communicating with you

If you follow these rules, you should be able to communicate with and understand your teenager a lot better. One word of warning: Just because you play by the rules, that doesn't mean that everyone will. There may be times when you will be blamed, your personality will be attacked, and so on. Hang in there! As an adult, you are older, wiser, and, we hope, more patient. Set a good example for your adolescent. Teach him what you know about the art of communicating. He'll appreciate it in the long run.

Contracting:
An Exercise in Give-and-Take

Open communication is important when dealing with an adolescent, but it's not a cureall. No matter how well you communicate, there are still bound to be some areas of disagreement left unresolved. Whether it be about the use of the car, proper curfew time, who does the household chores, or the amount of the weekly allowance, parents and teenagers often have *legitimate* differences of opinion. The subject matter of these disagreements, however, is not half as important as the manner with which they are handled. In this section, we will show you how to use contracting, an equitable and efficient approach to family problem-solving.

Contracting is unique in that nobody loses. When family members disagree, it's not uncommon for one or the other to "win" at the expense of the other. The problem with this, of course, is that hard feelings often crop up as an undesirable by-product. Contracting is a terrific way to avoid such hard feelings, and we're going to present you with an example here so you can see how it's done.

The W. Family:
A Case Study in Frustration

The W. family provided us with an outstanding example of how family members can make life miserable for each other. Donald, the sixteen-year-old boy, openly admitted that he couldn't stand his parents. According to him, his mother was a "witch" and his father just never "got off his case." Mr. and Mrs. W., however, saw things a little differently. They felt Donald was "bossy," "immature," and "just plain nasty." In their opinion, Donald was going out of his way to be, in their words, "defiant" and "impossible." We never doubted for even a moment that they all were upset with each other. The air in the office was crackling with tension as they poured out their complaints about each other to us. We listened patiently for a while, in order to let them get these things off their chests, and then we told them about contracting. We explained how and why contracting works, and then sent them home with their first family assignment.

Step Number One: The "Want List"

Basically, the Want List is exactly what its name implies. It's a list of behaviors you want from other members of your family. Notice that we used the word "behaviors." Vague terms, such as "respect" or "generosity" are not allowed. Instead, the Want List must be composed of specific *behaviors*. You can't observe "respect," for example, because it's an attitude. You can, however, observe and count those *behaviors* which contribute to "respect," such as saying "please" and "thank you," not using profanity, listening when the other person speaks, and so on. At any rate, we instructed each of the W.'s to make up a Want List of his own, and this is what they came up with.

Donald W.'s Want List

1. I want to use one of the family cars on Friday and Saturday nights, no questions asked.

2. I want to be able to wear my hair longer.
3. I want Mom and Dad to quit bugging me.
4. I want to be left alone in my room when I feel like being alone.
5. I want Dad not to holler at me every time I disagree with him.

Donald's Want List is really quite specific, except for Item Number 3. "Bugging" is a bit too vague, so we asked him what he meant by that term. As it turned out, "bugging" was simply Donald's word for criticism. Even more specifically, he felt his parents were overly critical of his schoolwork, his friends, and his taste in clothes and music. We thus amended Item 3 to read: "I want Mom and Dad to stop criticizing my schoolwork, friends, and taste in music and clothes." Now let's look at the Want List Mr. and Mrs. W. turned in.

MR. AND MRS. W.'S WANT LIST

1. We want no more backtalk from Donald.
2. We want no more profanity from Donald in our presence.
3. We want Donald to help more around the house.
4. We want Donald not to play his music so loud anymore.

This, too, is a very precise and straightforward Want List, although Item 3, just as on Donald's list, is somewhat vague. What could Donald do, in particular, that would qualify as "helping out more around the house"? Mr. and Mrs. W. agreed that if Donald helped with the dishes, made his bed each day, and mowed the lawn once a week, they would be satisfied. We therefore amended Item 3 to include those specific chores.

You'll notice that the W. family's problems now seem a lot more manageable. Just one week before they were calling each other names in our office. After compiling their Want List, however, they began to see their problems in terms of specific behaviors. We were now ready to plunge ahead with the second phase of the family contracting exercise.

Step Number Two: The Exchange

The exchange process is simply a trading of behaviors, sort of a "if you'll do this for me, I'll do that for you" arrangement. Sometimes it's a simple one-for-one behavior exchange; other times it's a two- or even three-for-one. Occasionally, family members simply agree to abide by each other's Want Lists, making only minor modifications here and there. Essentially, this is exactly what the W.'s did. All of their items seemed reasonable; *everyone* was pleased with the Exchange, and that's what's most important. We quickly moved on to the next step.

Step Number Three: Writing Up the Contract

It may seem a silly waste of time and energy to write up a formal contract, but we recommend it for two reasons. First, everyone is protected when the rules are laid down in writing. A clearly written contract removes any opportunity for one or both parties to make lame excuses or dispute the terms of the agreement. It's all there in the contract, spelled out in black and white. Second, there's something about a written contract that makes it more binding than a simple spoken agreement. Signing one's name to a written document seems to produce a greater sense of commitment to abiding by the terms of the agreement. At any rate, it's easy to do, and it increases the probability that all concerned will play by the rules. Here's what the W. family contract looked like. We recommend that you use a similar format when drawing up your own contracts.

THE W. FAMILY CONTRACT

We, the undersigned, agree to perform the following behaviors. If I, Donald W., will:

(1) not talk back to my parents,
(2) not use profanity in their presence,
(3) help with the dishes, make my bed each day, and mow the lawn once a week, and
(4) not play my record player at a volume objectionable to my parents,

then we, Mr. & Mrs. W., will do the following for Donald:

(1) let him use a car on Friday and Saturday nights, as long as he tells us where he's going,
(2) allow him to wear his hair longer,
(3) refrain from criticizing his schoolwork, friends, and taste in music and clothes,
(4) leave him alone in his room when he wants to be alone, and
(5) talk in a normal tone of voice when we disagree with him.

Signed _____

Date _____   Signed _____

Signed _____

Once the contract had been signed, we instructed the W.'s to post it on their refrigerator door. We also asked them to come in again the following week, so that we could review their progress with them.

Step Number Four: Modifying the Contract

The W.'s were noticeably pleased with themselves and each other when we next saw them. Each had tried hard to hold up his end of the bargain, and they reported getting along beautifully with each other as a result. There was one snag, however. The contract did not specify *exactly* how long Donald was allowed to wear his hair. After talking it over a few minutes, however, the W.'s agreed upon an appropriate length, and it was written into the contract. We also made it clear to the W.'s that if at any time any party should become dissatisfied with the contract, he or she was free to ask the other parties for a renegotiation of its terms. In short, we let them know that they hadn't signed their lives away, but that contract revisions were quite common and appropriate.

We called the W.'s six months later just to see how they were getting along. They told us that they had stuck to the original contract for about three months with great success. They had since discontinued it, however, feeling that living up to the contract had now become a habit for each of them, and as such, they no longer felt the need for the formal document. The W.'s also reported using contracting to successfully resolve two other issues which had arisen later. What's more, they had even shown another frustrated family exactly how it was done. Family contracting had definitely strengthened the W. family.

A Pause to Review

The point of this case example, aside from demonstrating how to use contracting, is to show you how simple it is to use. The W.'s eventually learned to contract with each other without relying on clinic help. In fact, they learned so well that they were able to help another family solve their problems via contracting. You, too, can master this important technique. Simply execute the following four basic steps:

1. Make up Want Lists of specific *behaviors* you'd like to see from each other.
2. Trade behaviors. Make sure *everyone* is satisfied.
3. Write up a formal contract, clearly stated and signed.
4. Modify the contract, if and when necessary.

What If Someone Breaks the Contract?

The W. family stuck with their contract. Each party adhered to the terms of the written agreement, and everyone was rewarded with a happier home life. Occasionally, however, someone will agree to a contract, and then fail to follow through. If this happens with your contract, don't panic. It's not a sign that contracting won't work in your home. A broken contract is usually a tip-off that too much was expected of someone too soon. An adolescent who's in the habit of swearing all the time, for example, may not be able to stop right away. What's required in a case like this is a *series* of contracts which *gradually* call for increasing amounts of behavior change.

The first contract might call for not more than four occurrences of swearing per day. Then, a week later, a new contract can be negotiated requiring three or fewer such occurrences. Proceeding in this step-wise fashion, you eventually reach zero. So, if someone violates your contract, it's probably because the contract was unrealistic to begin with. To say it again, behavior doesn't change overnight. It changes gradually. Thus, if your contract is broken, you can simply negotiate a new contract, this time taking *gradual* behavior changes into account.

What Contracting Means for You

As you've probably gathered by now, contracting is simply a formalized way of exchanging rewards between parents and adolescents. The behavior change of the teenager is rewarded by behavior change on the part of the parents, and vice versa. As we said earlier, everybody wins with contracting. Aside from the immediate reward value of behavior change, contracting offers several other benefits as well.

To begin with, the contracting exercise provides an excellent model for family communication. It focuses attention on specific behaviors and issues, rather than on the personalities of the family members involved. As such, name-calling and displays of temper occur less frequently.

Contracting also circumvents power struggles. Nobody "loses face" or is pressured into doing anything he cannot readily agree to do. Contracting provides a convenient way to solve problems without parents having to "crack down" or adolescents having to rebel.

Finally, contracting is a *family* exercise. It gets everyone working together to resolve common problems. In contracting, adolescents are treated like adults, and most of them appreciate that. By respecting the wishes and opinions of your youngster in this fashion, you'll earn a similar respect from him.

A Note to Parents on Attitude

Raising an adolescent can be hard work at times, but there are ways to make it easier. Perfecting communication skills and contracting are just two of those ways. Perhaps the most important thing for any parent to consider, however, is his or her *attitude*. Living with a teenager can be seen as a time of turbulence and dissatisfaction, or as a period of growth and new learning. It takes time and energy to raise children. It also takes a positive and constructive attitude, with a little patience thrown in for good measure. If you start "getting down" on your child, he'll be able to feel it. Adolescents need a little more space in which to grow than do younger kids. If they don't get that space, they're likely to become frustrated and rebellious. So give your teenager the benefit of the doubt when problems come up. He's growing up, and if you start treating him like an adult, he may even surprise you by starting to act like one.

10

The Slow Learner

WE WILL USE the term "slow learner" in a very general way. We will use it to describe a broad range of children with a wide variety of learning problems. The one thing all of these children have in common, however, is that their current level of functioning is significantly lower than other children their age. Looking at it in this way, the three-year-old who hasn't yet learned to talk and the ten-year-old who is failing in school can both be considered slow learners.

In a sense, this entire book has been devoted to learning. We have shown parents how to best *teach* their children more constructive behavior via the systematic application of rewards and punishments. The purpose of this chapter is to demonstrate how these same principles can be used to improve the performance of slow learners. In short, we are still teaching parents how to teach their children.

The Scope of This Chapter

This chapter does *not* contain everything you need to know about your youngster's learning problems. That's another book in and of itself. Without seeing your child, we can neither pretend to diagnose the source of his difficulties nor recommend specific remedial measures. For that, you'll have to consult a specialist. We can, however, offer you some basic teaching skills and techniques which are useful no matter what the specific problem may be.

Some Can't and Some Won't

We mentioned earlier that the term "slow learner" was a very general one, and as such, there are any number of factors which can contribute to learning difficulties in children. For example, retardation, organic brain damage, learning disabilities, hyperactivity, and behavior problems, just to name a few, can each, in its own way, impair a child's ability to function and learn adequately. Regardless of the nature of the problem, however, the outcome is the same. These youngsters find it hard to keep up with other kids their own age.

Given the wide variety of learning problems, any attempt to neatly categorize slow learners into separate groups is bound to be difficult. We make one distinction, however, which we find useful in determining our treatment strategies. There's a big difference between kids who *can't* do well and kids who *won't* do well. Let's explore this difference for a moment or two.

In the first group we find those children who lack the

ability to learn well, even though they may want to. They would like nothing better than to earn the rewards that come for good performance. They would love a report card with straight A's, but that's out of reach. They want to impress teachers and parents, but they simply can't. Because of a below-normal IQ, learning disability, or some other kind of impairment, these kids have two strikes against them before they even start. Learning is just plain harder for them than it is for the other children.

In contrast, there are children who possess the ability to do well, but simply lack *motivation*. For one reason or another, these kids simply don't want to learn badly enough. Poor motivation takes many forms. Some children can't stand the idea of doing their homework. Others would rather "cut up" in class or daydream than pay attention to what the teacher is saying. These are, however, potentially good learners in disguise. They're commonly called "underachievers." All this means is that they aren't really turned on by the typical rewards that go with good performance and high achievement. It may be more rewarding for them to watch TV, for example, than to work hard on homework assignments.

The major pitfall of making distinctions between "types" of children in this way is that there is usually quite a bit of overlap between groups. In other words, there are plenty of children who lack *both* ability and motivation. You may have heard about the "failure syndrome." It's a common affliction. A child may try hard to do well at first. One failure experience after another, however, soon convinces him that he's just wasting his time. His efforts to learn simply aren't being rewarded, so he directs most of his energies elsewhere. What's more, he develops a negative attitude toward learning in general. And why not? It's been anything but fun for him so far.

The Importance of a
Professional Examination

Reading this, you may be thinking, "All right, so you've divided slow learners into two categories, those who can't and those who won't. But just tell me one thing. How am I supposed to know where *my* child fits in? All I know for sure is that he doesn't do as well as the other kids." If you suspect that your child may be a slow learner, it's probably time to have him examined by a professional. First priority is given to a medical examination. It's important to know if the child's body is in good working order. More specifically, how's your child's vision? Is his hearing O.K.? Too often, learning problems are caused by sensory defects which go undetected for years. It's difficult to learn when you can't even see what's written on the blackboard or hear what the teacher is saying. Therefore, before you do anything else, arrange for your child to get a comprehensive physical examination.

Assuming that the medical exam rules out any physical problems, your next step should be to contact a competent psychologist. Tell him what the problem is and ask for a complete psychological workup. It is often difficult for parents to understand the meaning and significance of psychological test results. Many times the language is foreign to them and the concepts are unfamiliar. To help you get a better idea of exactly what your child's problem is, we've compiled a list of questions to ask the psychologist once he's examined your youngster. These questions are designed to get you some straight answers, couched in understandable and meaningful terms. Don't be afraid to ask them. It's for your child's sake that you do.

The Psychological Exam: Questions to Ask

1. How Complete Was the Testing?

The first thing a parent needs to know is the extensiveness of the psychological exam. Find out which tests the child was given and exactly what those tests are supposed to measure. We frequently encounter parents who get nothing more than an IQ estimate and a few achievement test scores from the testing. That's simply not sufficient. Those scores reflect what most parents are probably already aware of—that their child is a slow learner. If a learning disability is suspected, for example, the test battery should include the Illinois Test of Psycholinguistic Abilities (ITPA). This test pinpoints the source of a learning disability very effectively. There are other specific tests designed to diagnose brain damage, emotional problems, and so on. Make sure that all of the appropriate tests are included in the examination. If some are not, find out the reason why.

2. *How Does My Child Compare to Other Children His Age in Terms of Intellectual Functioning?*

An IQ score is just a number. Ask the tester to explain to you what that number means. It's helpful to know, for example, if your six-year-old is developing at the same rate as other six-year-olds, and if he isn't, it's also useful to know roughly how far behind he is.

3. *What, Specifically, Are My Child's Strengths and Weaknesses?*

This is crucial. Ask the examiner to enumerate those things your child càn do well, as well as those things which come harder for him. Press him to be specific. Some slow learners, such as retardates, are usually behind in almost every department. Others, however, may have problems in just one particular area of functioning. This is typically true for children with learning disabilities. Make sure that you know *exactly* what your child's strengths and weaknesses are.

4. *Was My Child Trying as Hard as He Could on the Tests?*

In other words, you want to know whether or not the test scores truly represent your child's capabilities. An experienced tester will be able to give you a pretty good estimate of this. Maybe the youngster was tired that day. Maybe he was bored. Perhaps his attention repeatedly wandered off the task at hand. Find these things out. If the examiner has reason to believe that the child didn't give it his best, you may want to have the testing done again later.

Of course, just finding out that your youngster didn't do as well as he could have is a very valuable piece of information in its own right. It may be a tip-off as to the way in which your child typically approaches his schoolwork.

5. *What Can I Expect from My Child in Terms of Current Behavior?*

Expectations of parents are important. There's no point in pushing your youngster to do things he's simply not ready for at the present time. That will only lead to frustration and resentment on both sides. On the other hand, if there are some things he's capable of doing but hasn't been, it's about time that he get started on them.

We recently saw a set of parents who had been told by the school that their five-year-old boy was retarded. Their initial response to this news had been one of despair and hopelessness. In a sense, they just threw in the towel and began letting their son do just about whatever he pleased. They were, in effect, giving up on him. What they were unaware of, however, was that the boy was capable of dressing himself, feeding himself, playing with other children, and so on. Even though he was retarded, there were still a lot of things he was capable of learning. Once his parents found out just what those things were, they set about the task of helping him function up to his potential. Today, that child is doing a lot more for himself than ever before, and his parents are tickled pink by his progress.

6. What Can I Expect in Terms of My Child's Future Development?

This is an important question. Some kinds of problems are typically outgrown; others are more permanent. It's imperative that you find out the limits, if any, on your child's potential. There's no use in harboring any false illusions, for example, if your child is severely retarded. On the other hand, there's no point in anguishing unnecessarily over your child's learning disability if your youngster's simply going to outgrow it in a few years.

This information is valuable from yet another standpoint. You can monitor your child's progress over the years to see if he's continuing to perform up to his capabilities. Periodic re-testing will also help you keep abreast of his development.

7. Is There Anything I Can Do to Help My Child Maximize His Potential?

This is the bread-and-butter question. Perhaps the only thing you can do is arrange for special schooling. If so, that's good to know. On the other hand, there may be a myriad of things you can do to help your youngster at home. Find out what these things are. Again, urge the examiner to be as specific as possible.

Mrs. H. came to us for some advice. She'd been informed by the school that her daughter had a learning disability in the realm of auditory reception. School personnel had advised her to work at home with the child on some "auditory training exercises." Well, her problem was that she just didn't know *specifically* what "auditory training exercises" to use. Was she supposed to read stories to her child? She didn't know. At any rate, we helped her compile a list of specific tasks appropriate to her daughter's age and disability. Once she knew *exactly* what to do, Mrs. H. was soon able to accelerate her daughter's learning progress.

A Warning about Psychological Testing

Assuming you get complete and honest answers to the questions we have just presented, you will be in possession of all of the information you need in order to deal effectively with your child's learning problems. Be careful, however, because this information can be misused as well. Too often parents will begin to treat their slow learner differently once they know he has a special problem. Some will begin to relate to the youngster as if he's some unusual creature from Mars. Others may begin to kill the kid with kindness or smother him with attention. The end result of any of these approaches is that the child begins to feel "different" from other people and, more often than not, inferior. You don't want that to happen. Be aware of how you behave toward your child. Just because certain things may come harder for him, he's not deserving of unusual treatment from you. Instead, work with the youngster so that he can develop to his potential, but aside from that, treat him the same as you would any other member of your family.

The Child Who
Wants to Learn but Cannot

As we stated earlier, the children in this category really want to do well. The problem is that they have been handicapped by some sort of learning impairment. For reasons they cannot help, these kids find it exceedingly difficult to master things as quickly as other children their own age. The task for the parents of children like this, therefore, is simply one of helping them to maximize their potential. No one can ask any more than that. A good psychologist can provide you with a number of learning exercises to do with your child at home. Tutoring your child in these exercises will require a good deal of your patience. The benefits to your child, however, more than justify this expenditure of time and energy. To help you to better help your youngster, we have assembled a set of general guidelines, which if closely followed should make learning at home easier and more pleasant for your child. Again, a psychologist who has seen and evaluated your child can better advise you on what specific exercises to use. The following guidelines are merely suggestions as to *how* you can best present those exercises to your child.

1. Make Learning Fun

If the home learning sessions are fun for your child, he'll try harder. Be creative. Make a game out of it. Get the youngster really involved by letting him *move* around, *touch* things, and so on. Many parents make the mistake of trying to force their children to sit quietly in one place for long periods of time. Well, that's just plain boring, and it makes those children more likely to resent the tutoring sessions. One more thing: Be sure that you smile a lot. Don't give the impression that the whole thing is just a big chore for you. If the child sees that you're having a good time, he's bound to feel better himself.

2. *Make Learning a Success Experience*

Slow learners have a history of failing, and they're sick of it. In fact, they're so used to failure that they often become reluctant to try anymore. Giving up easily can often become a way of life. It's up to you to see that this "failure syndrome" is replaced by a series of successes. Nothing generates enthusiasm quite as well as success.

Basically, there are two sure-fire methods to provide success experiences for your child. The first involves always starting each exercise at a level which the child can master easily, and then slowly progressing to more difficult items. If the task at hand is spelling, for example, begin by asking the child to spell words which you know he can spell correctly. After he gets a few successes tucked under his belt in this way, you can then gradually move up to words of increasing difficulty. Be sure he can spell correctly 70–80 percent of all words you ask—sprinkle the more difficult words in slowly. The second technique for promoting success is to start with the child's strengths, and then gradually shift to his weaknesses. If arithmetic is your child's forte, for example, start out the session with a few math problems. Once he has chalked up several correct answers in a row, he'll be ready to proceed to other subject areas in which he is less competent, such as reading or penmanship, for example.

3. Proceed in Small Steps

This is a point we have repeatedly emphasized throughout this book, and you're probably tired of hearing it. Nevertheless, we're going to say it again. Don't expect too much too soon, especially from a slow learner. Proceed through the material in a logical, step-wise fashion, making sure that the child masters the material at each step before moving on to the next. If you push a youngster too far too quickly, he's only going to start making mistakes, and, on top of that, he'll begin to resent the whole thing. Let his performance dictate the pace of the learning sessions.

4. Praise Heavily

In Chapter Three, we outlined in detail for you the essential components of praise. Here's your chance to really get some practice at it. Praise your child liberally, not only for successes but also for *trying*. Many children would prefer to play with friends or watch TV rather than work on home learning exercises. Therefore, see to it that your child is amply rewarded just for showing up. Even if he's struggling with the material, you can say things like "You're really working hard today" or "It makes me so happy when you really try like that." Of course, criticism for errors is definitely a "no-no." If the youngster makes a mistake, you can even go so far as to soften the blow by saying, "That was a tough one, wasn't it?" or "Even the big kids have a hard time with some of these." Learning should become a positive experience for your child. You can make it that way by praising him every chance you get.

Some kids find it awfully difficult to sit still for more than several minutes at a time. If that description fits your child, you may have to supplement your praise with some additional rewards. You can give the youngster frequent rest breaks, for example. Make him earn these breaks, however, by working on a certain number of learning exercises first. You can even make up a reward menu, like the ones discussed in Chapter Eight, and then let the child choose his own rewards for working so hard. Keep in mind, however, that the youngster must *earn* these rewards. He should do the work first, *before* he gets rewarded. Also, be sure that you reward *effort* and not just correct answers. If you can encourage the child to work hard in this way, the right answers will begin to come sooner or later.

5. Make Learning Interesting

Nobody likes to do the same old thing day in and day out. Your child is no exception. You can help keep him from getting bored by being creative. Change the learning exercises and tasks frequently. Use exciting learning materials. Audio-visual aids are great sustainers of interest. Whenever possible, use materials the child can touch and manipulate. Also, don't be afraid to take your learning sessions out of the home. Parks, zoos, museums, are terrific places for children to learn more about the world they live in. There's an added dividend derived from these activities as well—they tend to bring families closer together. So spend some time now and then just thinking about ways to inject a little more gusto into the learning sessions. You are limited in this only by your own ingenuity.

6. Let Your Child Do the Tasks

It often requires a lot of patience and self-control to sit by and watch a youngster grapple with a problem. By all means, however, let the child try to figure it out for himself. *He's* the one who needs the practice, not you. Besides, if the child does manage to conquer a tough problem all by himself, he's going to feel a heck of a lot better about his accomplishment than if you helped him with it. This same principle can be applied to all facets of your child's life. Permit your child to tie his own shoes, for example, even though it might be a lot quicker and easier if you did it for him. A child learns best by doing. Don't deprive him of the practice he needs to improve and develop.

A Mrs. D. asked us for some coaching. It seems that she had been tutoring her son Tom at home for over a year, but in that time his performance in school had remained essentially unchanged. She just couldn't understand why. Things he has seemingly mastered at home were still giving him a lot of trouble in the classroom. Well, it turns out that Tom hadn't really been mastering anything at home. Mrs. D. had been doing what we call "overcoaching." That is, whenever Tom would get stuck on a problem, even momentarily, she would quickly intervene and show him how to solve it. In effect, *she* was the one who was mastering the homework. Tom was really no more than an interested observer. Once Mrs. D. began to let Tom do his own work, however, his performance in school began to improve.

7. Be a Good Example

Children like to imitate the behavior of adults, especially their parents. They look up to their parents and want to be more like them. That, of course, places a responsibility directly on parents to model desirable behavior. If you'd like your child to read more books, for example, let him see that you read books, too. In the same vein, you can't expect your child to learn the proper use of the English language if your own utterances are filled with grammatical errors. Try to become more aware of your own behavior and the example it is setting for your child. Remember, you're being watched.

8. Choose a Location Suitable for Learning

Most children are easily distracted. For that reason, you need to work with your child in a room free of other people, pets, TV, and excessive noise. In order to get the most out of the home exercises, your youngster must be able to give them his undivided attention. Frequent interruptions will only impede his progress. Of course, we don't mean to imply that your lessons should be conducted in the laundry room or closet. The surroundings should be as pleasant as possible, featuring comfortable chairs, ample work space, and good lighting. Just make sure, however, that the exercise area you choose is conducive to maximum effort and learning.

Summing Up

We have presented you with a list of eight suggestions to help your child get the most out of the home learning sessions. These suggestions are research validated and guaranteed effective, regardless of the specific type of exercises being used. Here they are again, this time in simplified form.

Learning Aids for Slow Learners

1. Make learning fun
2. Make learning a success experience
3. Proceed in small steps
4. Praise heavily
5. Make learning interesting
6. Let your child do the tasks
7. Be a good example
8. Choose a location suitable for learning

As you've probably noticed, this list of suggestions draws heavily from material presented earlier in this book. We have pulled together those principles which we feel to be especially appropriate for slow learners with *ability* deficits. In the next section of this chapter, we will turn our attention to those children who lack the *motivation* to learn and do well in school.

What Is a Motivation Problem?

Motivation problems come in all shapes and sizes. The child who doesn't do his homework, the child who refuses to participate in class discussions, the child who daydreams, and the child who "cuts up" in class can all be considered as having motivation problems. What's the common denominator? They all find school work and/or school activities *less rewarding* than other nonrelated activities. It may just be more fun for the child to watch

TV, for example, than to complete his math assignments. Or it may be more enjoyable for the child to talk to classmates than to pay attention to what the teacher has to say about current events. Regardless of how the problem manifests itself, however, the remedy is surprisingly simple—increase the rewards available to the child for learning and doing his schoolwork. That's usually all it takes.

Of course, the school has primary responsibility for motivating your child to learn. More specifically, the teacher has first-hand control over rewards and punishments in the classroom. It is up to the teacher, for example, to make class assignments interesting. It is the teacher who must discipline your child when he's acting up, draw him out when he doesn't want to contribute to class discussions, or simply prompt him to pay attention or get to work. There are two things parents can do, however, to assist the teacher. They can (1) help motivate the child to work on his homework, and (2) they can reward the child for working hard in school. Using a case example, we'll show you how to accomplish these goals with maximum efficiency.

An Educational Success Story

The parents of eleven-year-old Artie T. were distraught. Their son was failing in school, and on top of that he really didn't seem to care. Although he had been a good student during his first two years of school, his grades had gotten progressively worse since that time. Psychological testing revealed that Artie was, in fact, a very bright boy, and there was no evidence from the tests to suggest any learning disabilities or other impairments. Actually,

Artie's teacher had known for some time what the real source of the problem was. Artie just wasn't doing any schoolwork. He goofed off in class every chance he got, and although she didn't know what he'd been doing at home, she did know for sure that it was not homework. As far as the teacher could tell, Artie's problem was one of poor motivation, and she referred Mr. and Mrs. T. to us for some assistance.

We decided to tackle the homework problem first, since the T.'s had more control over what Artie did at home than what he did at school. For a long time, Mr. and Mrs. T. hadn't really paid very much attention to whether or not Artie did his homework. Sure, they asked him now and then if his homework had been completed, and, whenever they did, he invariably responded that it had. They usually just took his word for it, and as a result, they let him go outside and play with friends, watch TV, or do whatever else he wanted to do. Needless to say, Mr. and Mrs. T. had been somewhat surprised to find out later that Artie had, in fact, been deceiving them. Angry because they had been lied to, Mr. and Mrs. T. then decided to crack down. Artie was forced to sit in his room for at least two hours every night and work on class assignments. After no more than a few days of this, however, Artie got wise and simply began reading comics and listening to the radio during this time. To be sure, he faithfully put in his two hours every night, but his homework was still being neglected. Artie's parents were at a loss for what to do next, and it was at this point that Artie's teacher sent them to see us. Here is how we dealt with Artie's homework problem in a logical and stepwise fashion.

Step 1: Defining the Problem

Our first step consisted of simply explaining to Artie's parents what a motivation problem was in layman's terms. Artie currently was not being rewarded sufficiently for completing his homework each night. Evidently, good grades and teacher approval were simply not enough to get him working. The solution to the problem, as we saw it, was one of increasing the rewards available to Artie for performing this task.

Step 2: Finding a Suitable Work Area

It was hard for Artie to do homework in his bedroom. There were just too many fun things for him to do in there. Thus, we recommended that Mr. and Mrs. T. find a place where Artie could devote his energies *exclusively* to his homework. They finally decided on the dining-room table as the best spot. The lighting was good, the noise level was low, there was ample work space, and, most important, the room was free of potentially distracting activities.

Step 3: A Special Incentive Program

We next set about the task of implementing a special incentive program for Artie. Essentially, we followed the same procedures as those outlined in Chapter Eight of this book. We won't rehash that material, but we do recommend that you read that chapter again before designing a home program of your own. In that way, you can guard against omitting any important steps.

Basically, we instructed Mr. and Mrs. T. in how to reward Artie's study behavior with activities and privileges.

In designing this program, we gave special emphasis to the following considerations:

1. Making sure the reward menu was appealing to Artie. In other words, was he willing to work for the items on the menu?
2. *Gradually* increasing the time Artie spent on homework each night. Artie's parents were cautioned against pushing him to do too much too soon.
3. Periodic praising of Artie *while* he was studying. No one likes to sit all by himself in a room for too long. We thus encouraged Mr. and Mrs. T. to check on Artie every once in a while and praise him for working hard.
4. The concept of *immediate* reward was emphasized. Grades are very distant rewards. Rewarding Artie each night following completion of his homework time served to strengthen his new study habits and bridge the time gap between grading periods.

Step 4: Evaluating the Child's Progress

Artie's teacher confirmed for us that his grades were rising. According to her, his homework was now being done promptly and well. Hence, we concluded that Artie's special incentive program had, in fact, accomplished what it was designed to do. The teacher also reported to us, however, that Artie was still acting up in class and that this was keeping him from paying attention to classroom exercises. She felt that if Artie could only begin to behave himself a little better and devote more of his energy to class assignments, he would finally be able to perform up to his potential. This turned out to be just the information we needed to begin phase two of our work with Artie. We also dealt with this problem in a logical, step-wise manner, very similar to our approach to the home-work issue. Here's what we did:

Step A: Defining the Problem

Since the behaviors we wanted to change were occurring *at school*, we felt it wise to invite Artie's teacher to join with his parents in the planning phase of our problem-solving. She was eager to help us out any way she could, as Artie's classroom be-havior was beginning to make teaching her class more difficult.

We defined the problem, that of Artie's not doing any work at school, in terms of *competing rewards*. We explained that Artie's payoff for talking to class-mates, making faces, getting out of his seat, and so on, was simply the *attention* of his classmates and the teacher. The other kids loved it when he clowned around, and they rewarded his efforts with lots of laughter and friendly interaction. Artie's teacher, although not quite such a big fan of Artie's, had nevertheless been *inadvertently* rewarding Artie's behavior with her attention. By repeatedly bawling him out in front of the other kids, she was, in effect, making him a star. He was the center of everyone's attention all at once, and he loved it.

The solution to the problem thus lay in decreasing the amount of rewarding attention that Artie got for clowning, while at the same time increasing the re-wards for working hard on class assignments. In order to do this, we needed the cooperation of the parents, the teacher, and, most of all, Artie. We got it.

Step B: Implementing the Program

To decrease the amount of attention being paid to Artie's goofing off, we instructed the teacher in how to use *time out*. As soon as he started to clown around, Artie's teacher would immediately send him to the time-out area. No more big fuss over Artie. All he got instead was a quiet but firm removal from the limelight. He didn't even get a chance to savor the laughs. When the five minutes in time out had elapsed, Artie was allowed to return to his seat. If he started in again, he was simply shipped back to time out forthwith.

Time out worked well, but it was really only half the solution. Time out taught Artie what he was *not* supposed to do. We implemented a special incentive program to help him learn what *to* do instead. Again, we followed the steps outlined in Chapter Eight. This particular program, however, had an interesting variation. Artie earned points *in school* for spending predetermined amounts of time working quietly in his seat. The teacher kept track of these points on a slip of paper each day. At the end of the day, she would sign the point slip and send it home with Artie. *At home*, then, Artie could cash in his points for items from the reward menu, such as play time with friends, special desserts, and so on. At the same time, both the parents and teacher were instructed in the art of effective praising as outlined in Chapter Three. The teacher was en-

couraged to praise Artie frequently and heavily
whenever he was "on-task" in class. Artie's parents
were instructed to praise him often, especially when
he cashed in his points at the end of the day. Neither
the parents nor the teacher were to criticize him at
any time for not earning points. That was to be
Artie's business, not theirs. If Artie came home with
a blank slip, his parents were not permitted to comment on this at all.

Step C: Evaluating the Program

Phase Two of the program was a tremendous success. Artie was earning lots of points for working
hard in the classroom. Also, after no more than five
brief stopovers in time out, his clowning behavior
had virtually disappeared. He had now turned into
a model student, and gradually, over the course of
the next semester, his grades had risen to the point
where he had become a consistent B+ student. All
that remained to be done was the phasing out of the
special incentive programs. As it turned out, this
presented no problems. Artie had gotten "hooked"
on doing well, so he had no difficulties in sustaining
his motivation and desire to learn once the special
programs were terminated. Also, his parents had
gotten into the habit of consistently praising him
for appropriate behavior, and Artie really appre-
ciated that.

Teachers Are Your Best Allies

We presented Artie's success story because it involved both home and school behaviors. The special incentive program for homework was easily implemented by Artie's parents. The program which dealt with Artie's behavior in school, however, required the teacher's cooperation and assistance. Without her help, there's no way the program would have worked. So, if your child has been experiencing difficulties in school, consult with his teacher and cooperate with her actively. Too often, parents of problem children can make life miserable for the teacher. You want that teacher on your side, not working against you. When she gives that extra effort required to really help your child, let her know you appreciate it. We all need a little recognition now and then, just to keep on doing what we're doing. Teachers are no exception.

Tying It All Together

In this chapter, we have outlined for you some techniques designed to enhance the progress of slow learners. To begin with, we provided some suggestions on how to help a child with an ability deficit get the most out of home tutoring sessions. Then we looked at ways for parents to "light a fire" under kids with motivation problems. As we mentioned earlier, there are a number of children who lack not only the ability but who also lack the inclination to learn and do well. Parents of these kids can draw from *all* of the material presented in this chapter. By this time, assuming that you have read this book carefully and followed through on the various exercises included, you should be fairly expert in the ways of encouraging positive behavior change. You probably know enough now to be able to custom-tailor home programs and strategies to fit your particular situation exactly. Don't be afraid to be creative. If you've mastered the fundamentals, you'll probably be quite effective no matter what particular approach you happen to choose. We have confidence in this material, and we have confidence in you, as well.

11 ◆§ ੩◆

The Withdrawn and Fearful Child

See if any of these situations sound familiar to you.

1. The doorbell rings. It's some old friends of yours from across town. As you show them in, your little boy takes one worried look and then scampers out of the room.

2. It's such a beautiful day that you've decided to take your family to the beach. Your little three-year-old, however, refuses to go anywhere near the water. When you take her by the hand and attempt to walk with her in the shallow water, she begins to scream, kick, and cry.

3. You and your spouse have been in bed for about an hour. Lo and behold, you notice the bedroom door beginning to creak as it slowly opens. Your little boy sticks his head in the room, and in a whisper announces that there are "creatures and

ghosts" in his bedroom. He wants to sleep in your bed again tonight.

4. Your daughter has been wearing a worried expression on her face for the past three weeks. On top of that, she's been asking "Do you love me?" at least five times a day.

5. You've grown another shadow. Your four-year-old has become your constant companion, following you from room to room throughout the house. Even though he occasionally leaves your side to play with friends outside, he regularly comes indoors just to make sure you're still nearby.

6. A bunch of kids are playing together in your yard. All but one are involved in a game of tag. The one exception is your youngster. He's playing by himself again in the sandbox.

The preceding scenes depict behaviors common to the withdrawn and/or fearful child. If your child is prone to behaving similarly to one or more of these descriptions, this chapter should be of special interest to you. We're going to show you some proven ways to help your child overcome his fears and insecurities, whatever they may be.

Whose Problem Are We Talking About?

Most of this book has dealt with child behaviors that are often bothersome to parents. This chapter, along with the previous one, therefore, represents somewhat of a departure. Here we are concerned with problems that belong to the child *alone*. He has to live with the fear, shyness, or insecurity, not you. Of course, we recognize that loving parents want to help their children in any way they can, and that's why we have included a chapter on this topic. Just keep in mind, however, that we're dealing now with the child's problem. Your role is thus simply that of a concerned helper who only wants the best for the child.

The Causes of Fear

Usually a child will exhibit fear in a situation simply because he suspects that the situation may hold punishing consequences for him. The youngster who fears dogs, for example, is probably worried about the possibility of being bitten, a punishing consequence. The "clinging" child, the one who rarely lets his parents out of his sight, is most likely afraid of the punishing consequences of being abandoned. The shy child who runs from strangers may not want to experience the embarrassment or discomfort of having to interact with new people. In order to help these children overcome their fears, then, one has to somehow persuade them or, better yet, show them that their fears are unfounded, i.e., that the consequences are not, in fact, punishing but rewarding instead.

General Guidelines to Mastering Fear

There are some general procedures which parents can use to help their kids master all kinds of fear-producing situations. We will present these first, and then go on to show you later on in the chapter how these procedures can be applied to a wide variety of more specific problems. But first, let's take a look at the basic guidelines.

1. Stay Calm

Quite often parents will react with alarm when they find out that their child is fearful. That only makes matters worse. If the child sees that you're upset, he's going to feel even worse about himself. Brothers and sisters may begin to tease him for being a "fraidy cat." If the child sees that everyone around him considers him unusually fearful, before long he will begin to believe it himself. And once that happens, he'll be even more prone to behaving that way. Therefore, if you can, try to keep a level head about your child's problem. If he's shy, for example, it's not the end of the world. Besides, you can help him change all that.

2. Deal with Only One Behavior at a Time

Throughout this book, we have encouraged parents to be specific. Defining situations in terms of *specific behaviors* is essential to problem-solving. Try to pinpoint the exact nature of your child's fears. Defining the problem in vague terms, such as "shyness" or "insecurity," just won't do. "Hiding from strangers" or "refusing to play with other children" are much more manageable descriptions. Behavioral definition gives you something concrete and observable to work with.

Also, once the key behaviors have been pinpointed and defined, deal with them *one at a time*. If your child is afraid of dogs, cats, water, and "ghosts," for example, pick just *one* of those fears to start with. Only when that problem is solved can you move on to another. Besides, the child may develop a new sense of competency and self-esteem from conquering the first fear, which then will make it easier for him to deal with the others.

3. *Avoid Sudden or Intense Exposures*

You've probably heard the proverbial story about the father who taught his little boy to swim by taking him out in a rowboat and then tossing him in the water. Well, this "sink-or-swim" philosophy has probably caused a lot of anguish for frightened youngsters. The effects of a sudden or intense exposure to a fear-arousing situation can be devastating. A confused and panicked child is simply not in a position to master his fear rationally. His primary concern instead will be to get himself out of that situation and never come back. In short, sudden or intense exposures will all too often accomplish nothing and are likely to only make matters worse, thus disappointing both you and the child in the process.

4. *Proceed Gradually in Small Steps*

The alternative to the sudden or intense exposure is simply gradual, step-by-step exposure. This allows the child to experience mastery at every point along the way. It also gives him time to become familiar with the circumstances and conditions surrounding the feared situation. Only then can he rationally determine for himself that there's really nothing to be afraid of. It also provides him with *practice* in the new behaviors you're trying to teach. If your child is afraid of the dark, for example, let him *gradually* get used to increasing increments of darkness *over time*. Locking him in a totally darkened room will only impede his progress.

5. *Praise the Child for Every Success*

As we mentioned earlier, parents can help by showing the child that the feared situation is rewarding rather than punishing. Lots of praise is vital to that process. Praise the youngster heavily each time he makes some progress, regardless of how small the gain. As long as he's trying his best, your child deserves your support.

Conversely, it also makes sense for parents to avoid criticism. Remember, this is the child's problem, not yours. Criticism will serve no other purpose than to make him feel inadequate. If the child fails at some point along the way, you'll just have to break the program down into smaller steps. Make sure that success occurs at every step of the way and that each success is followed by a substantial amount of praise, affection, and attention from you.

6. *Ignore Fear Statements*

Children will often verbalize their fears even when not directly confronted with the feared situation. If you respond to these statements with lots of attention and sympathy, you are, in effect, simply rewarding that kind of behavior. For this reason, we recommend that you ignore, as much as possible, these kinds of statements. The idea behind this is to withdraw support for fearful verbalizations and then reward statements which indicate more positive thinking. The child who gets into the habit of saying "I can't" is less likely to succeed than the child who says "I can."

We don't mean to imply that you should simply turn your back each time your child brings up his concerns or fears. When he begins to say the same old things repeatedly, however, then it's time to do something about that. Otherwise, your child will convince himself in this way that he is unable to master the feared situation.

7. Make Expectations Clear

You can help prepare your child to confront a feared situation simply by telling him what to expect. Using the fear of dogs as an example again, you might tell the child that a dog may try to lick him with his tongue, wag his tail, bark, or even jump up on him. Forewarned in this way, the child will then be less likely to be surprised and frightened by the dog's behavior. In the same way, you can tell a shy child to expect that guests will probably say hello to him, shake his hand, and perhaps chat for a little while with him. Knowing what to expect will then make it easier for the youngster to overcome his fear of strangers.

One more point: Be sure that you radiate confidence while you outline these expectations for your child. Behave as if you're totally convinced that the youngster will handle the situation effectively now that he knows what to expect. Positive thinking is contagious.

8. Have Patience

Behavior change is usually gradual. Therefore, you will need to be patient. Remember, even though the child's fears may seem irrational or silly to you, they're very real to him. Don't push him to do too much too soon. Let him set the pace. Let him tuck a few minor successes under his belt before coaxing him on to total mastery. Again, it's the child's problem. If he's willing to be patient, you can be, too.

A Pause to Review

Let's take a moment or two here to summarize what we've covered so far. We've given you some general guidelines to follow in helping your child overcome his fears and/or insecurities. Here they are again in list form.

Dealing with Fears: Some General Tips

1. Stay calm
2. Deal with *one* behavior at a time
3. Avoid sudden or intense exposures
4. Proceed gradually in small steps
5. Praise the child for every success
6. Ignore fear statements
7. Make expectations clear
8. Have patience

Parents who keep these considerations in mind should have no problems in encouraging their children to deal more effectively with their fears. In the beginning of this chapter we promised to show you how these guidelines could be applied to specific problems. We opened the chapter with six common "fear situations." We didn't make them up. They are taken from actual case descriptions in our clinic files. Each of these cases was successfully resolved using the techniques and strategies we have presented so far. We feel that the best way for you to learn how to deal with your child's problems is simply to observe the way we handled these situations. Although these case examples are in all likelihood not perfect replicas of your particular situation, one or more of them should be similar enough to give you a pretty good idea of how best to proceed.

Shyness

Shyness is often inadvertently rewarded by parents and other adults. You're probably familiar with the old maxim "Children should be seen and not heard." Well, like most philosophies in a nutshell, this one belongs in a nutshell. Children have a right to express themselves and be heard. If they can't, they are being cheated out of an important aspect of growing up. An unusually shy child is bound to have problems adjusting in school and other new and different situations in his life. We will present for you here two cases in which parents were successful in helping their children overcome shyness. One involves shyness with adults. The other deals with a child who was shy only in the presence of other children.

Case #1: Shyness with Adults

Mr. and Mrs. W. came to us for some help with their son's shyness. Four-year-old Brucie was prone to scurrying out of the living room whenever guests came over to visit. Since Brucie would be starting school in the fall, Mr. and Mrs. W. felt it was about time he got over this excessive shyness and got used to meeting and talking to other adults. Here are the steps that were taken to resolve this problem:

1. PROBLEM DEFINITION

It's hard to work with problems couched in such vague terms as shyness. Thus, our first step consisted of defining the problem in terms of a specific behavior, i.e., getting Brucie to interact with house guests and other adults.

2. MAKING EXPECTATIONS CLEAR

We instructed Mr. and Mrs. W. to "warn" Brucie of expected company *before* they arrived. In that way, he wasn't likely to be surprised or caught off guard when they arrived. We also encouraged them to exude confidence and enthusiasm about a visit from friends while they explained to Brucie what they wanted him to do.

3. PROCEEDING GRADUALLY IN SMALL STEPS

Since Brucie had been hiding from visitors for so long, we knew it would be unreasonable to expect him to change his behavior completely overnight. Thus, a plan was devised to allow Brucie to gradually increase his exposure to company over a period of several weeks. We programed that exposure in a series of small steps. Brucie was not to proceed to the next step until the previous one had been mastered at least twice. Here are those steps in sequence:

- To begin with, Brucie was instructed to say *only* "hello" to the guests. After that, he was free to leave the room if he wanted. After mastering step one on two separate occasions, Brucie was then asked to say "hello" *and* shake hands. Once he had done this, he could do whatever he wished. The third step required Brucie to say "hello," shake hands, and then remain in the room with the guests for at least five minutes. His parents told him, however, that he was not required to talk with, or even look at, the guests once he had greeted them. After satisfactorily carrying out the five-minute requirements two times in a row, the time span was then increased to ten minutes. It was at this point that the major breakthrough occurred. On one occasion, after saying "hello," shaking hands, and playing quietly in the room for several minutes, Brucie suddenly picked up one of his toys and took it over to one of the guests. He and the guest quickly got into a conversation about the toy, and before long they had become great pals. Since that time, Brucie has been growing increasingly comfortable interacting with new people.

- In short, by being *gradually* exposed to new faces in this way, he was able to discover for himself how rewarding such interactions could be.

4. Praising Brucie for Each Success

Mr. and Mrs. W. were encouraged to praise Brucie lavishly each time he mastered one of the program steps. Furthermore, this was to be done *as soon as possible* after he completed the required behaviors, even if it meant seeking him out in another room. They simply explained to their guests what they were doing and then excused themselves for a moment to go and praise Brucie. This procedure usually took less than a minute of their time, but it paid off handsomely. Also, since they role-played with us the proper use of the praising technique, their praising was doubly effective.

5. EXPANDING THE PROBLEM TO OTHER HOMES

Once Brucie had become thoroughly comfortable with strangers in his own home, we felt it was time to work on his shyness in the homes of other people. Basically, the same steps were followed, and the results were the same. Brucie became an outgoing and lively child in the presence of adults, and the entire procedure took less than six weeks.

Case #2: Shyness with Other Children

Jeremy C. was a loner. His parents told us that he rarely played with other children, regardless of what they were doing. Even if the other kids happened to be playing a game in his own yard, Jeremy would typically occupy himself by playing quietly away from the group. Our remedy for the problem went as follows:

1. DEFINING THE PROBLEM

In specific behavioral terms, the problem was simply one of getting Jeremy to interact more often with other children.

2. PROCEEDING GRADUALLY IN SMALL STEPS

Jeremy's mother arranged to have a neighbor boy named Bobby come over to the house each day. Bobby was Jeremy's own age, and they shared a lot of similar interests. At first, they tended to play separately, but Mrs. C. kept *gently* encouraging them to do various things together. In this way, they slowly but surely got used to each other, and eventually they became the best of friends. At this point, Mrs. C. began to invite yet another youngster over to join Bobby and Jeremy. Before long, she was gradually adding more and more children to the new play group. They began to do all sorts of things together, such as playing games, watching TV, drawing, sharing refreshments, and so on, and Jeremy was right in the thick of it. By *slowly* introducing Jeremy to the rewards of playing with other kids, Mrs. C. had made it possible for him to become friendly with almost every kid on the block.

3. PRAISING JEREMY FOR HIS SUCCESSES

Each time she noticed Jeremy playing with Bobby or one of the other children, Mrs. C. made it a point to praise *both* of them for playing so well together. Of course, having fun with the other kids eventually became a big reward for Jeremy in its own right.

Phobias

Phobias are commonly defined as irrational fears. Children can become deathly afraid of almost anything, whether it be dogs, water, "ghosts," or bugs. As an adult you can see that these fears are irrational, i.e., that there's really no reason for the child to be afraid, but that sure doesn't make that fear any less real to the youngster. We're going to show you here how we "cured" one child's fear of water and another's fear of "ghosts." The same procedures we applied to the water and "ghost" phobias can be used to deal effectively with almost every kind of phobia you may encounter.

Case #3: The Fear of Water

Janet M., according to her parents, had this terrible fear of water. While other kids her age were learning how to swim, for some reason or another Janet wouldn't even consent to go wading. Mr. and Mrs. M. were worried that Janet might be "emotionally disturbed."

1. DEFINING THE PROBLEM

We quickly dispelled the possibility of "emotional disturbance." In simple language, Janet was simply afraid of the water and nothing more. In fact, she really wasn't even afraid of water, since she had never complained about taking baths, sitting in her little backyard pool, or being out in the rain. Her problem, defined in behavioral terms, thus was that she feared something might happen to her if she went into the nearby lake.

2. MAKING EXPECTATIONS CLEAR

We instructed Janet's parents to take her to the beach every day for the next week. If Janet resisted, she was to be told that she didn't have to go in the water, but that she did have to accompany the rest of the family on these outings.

3. IGNORING FEAR STATEMENTS

Furthermore, Janet's parents were encouraged to give her a lot of positive attention while at the beach. No references were to be made, however, to her fear of the water. If *she* happened to mention it, her statements were to be ignored. We role-played the proper ignoring procedure with Mr. and Mrs. M., just to make sure that they were maximally effective in its use. Of course, if Janet at any time said something remotely favorable about the beach and/or the water, she was to be praised immediately. We role-played this procedure as well.

4. PROCEEDING GRADUALLY IN SMALL STEPS

The proposed plan of action was really quite elementary. It involved simply having one or both of Janet's parents play with her in the sand and slowly but surely move the play closer and closer to the water. Since they were going to be at the beach for seven days, there was to be no rush on how fast they would proceed.

Once the pressure to go in the water was removed, Janet felt a lot better about going to the beach. In fact, she was wading by the third day. Mr. and Mrs. M. had followed instructions carefully. In short, they had made it fun for Janet to be at the beach. They made sand castles and moats with her. They dug large holes in the sand and filled them with water for Janet to play in. She loved it. All the while, however, they were inching closer to the water. The turning point really came on the third day, when Janet began running down to the water, of her own accord, to fill her little bucket. Before she knew it she was standing in the water and not minding it one bit.

5. PRAISING JANET FOR SUCCESSES

Mr. and Mrs. M. were not stingy with their praise and attention. They consistently and enthusiastically praised Janet for coming with them to the beach, for playing well in the sand, and, of course, for finally going in the water. Today Janet is an excellent swimmer, and a happy and healthy little girl. What was that we heard about "emotional disturbance"?

Case #4: A Fear of "Ghosts"

Candy M. had made a startling discovery. Her bedroom was infested with "ghosts" and "creatures." This didn't bother her much during the daytime, but it sure got scary at night. As a result, she had been creeping into her parents' bedroom lately and asking if she could sleep with them. The first couple of times this happened, Mr. and Mrs. M. thought the whole thing was really rather cute, and so they permitted her to come into their bed. When it became apparent to them that this was becoming a nightly ritual, however, they felt they had better put a stop to it. The problem was, though, that Candy wasn't about to cooperate. She liked the new regime. After several weeks of hassling with her and futilely trying to convince her that there were no "ghosts" and "creatures" in her room, two very tired parents came to us for some help. Here's how we got Candy back to sleeping in her own room.

1. DEFINING THE PROBLEM

In behavioral terms, the problem was simply one of getting Candy to sleep in her own bed the entire night.

2. MAKING EXPECTATIONS CLEAR

Mr. and Mrs. M. were instructed to let Candy know exactly what they expected from her in terms of her bedtime behavior. From now on, she was to sleep in her own bed, and that was that. To help make that prospect less frightening for her, though, they agreed to let Candy sleep with a night light and keep her bedroom door open. At first, Candy didn't like the idea, but she said she'd try.

3. IGNORING FEAR STATEMENTS

Mr. and Mrs. M. had fallen into a common parenting trap. They had repeatedly tried to explain to Candy that there was simply no reason for her to be afraid. Well, Candy wasn't about to be persuaded. In fact, all the attention she got for this seemed to be inadvertently rewarding her fearfulness. We suggested a new approach. From now on, Candy's fear statements were to be ignored. No more sympathy and nonproductive explanations. If Candy came into their bedroom at night, for example, one of her parents would simply get out of bed and escort Candy back to her room *without a word*. We role-played the ignoring technique with Mr. and Mrs. M., so that they could be maximally effective with it.

4. PRAISING CANDY FOR HER SUCCESSES

Candy's parents were instructed to praise her enthusiastically each morning for sleeping in her own bed. To bolster the power of their praising, we practiced this technique with them. Furthermore, if Candy went the whole night without bothering her parents, she was also given her choice of breakfast foods on the following morning. Since Candy adored "Pop Tarts," this bonus treat really pleased her.

After just four days of the new program, Candy ceased her midnight meanderings. Once Mr. and Mrs. M. had adopted a *firm* and *consistent* bedtime policy, it didn't take Candy long to realize that sleeping in her parents' bed was simply no longer a possibility. This points up an important consideration when dealing with bedtime behaviors. Don't get caught up in bedtime rituals. You have to draw the line for a child sooner or later, so it might as well be sooner. Once you have decided on a particular course of action, stick with it. If you give in to your child's wishes, even just a few times, you're only setting yourself up for hassles later on.

Insecurity

Insecurity can take many forms. The following case examples highlight two very common varieties. The first describes a child who seemingly was not convinced that her parents loved her. The second involves a "clinger," a child who relentlessly followed his mother around the house all day. Both problems were successfully resolved once the parents learned to systematically redistribute the social rewards at their disposal.

Case #5: Do You Love Me?

Eight-year-old Anita R. had begun to sound like a broken record. At least six times each day she would ask one of her parents the same old question—"Do you love me?" At first, Mr. and Mrs. R. had been rather pleased by this behavior. They assumed that it meant that Anita really cared for them deeply. Therefore they responded to this questioning with lots of physical affection and detailed explanations of how much they loved her. Apparently, Anita wasn't satisfied with those explanations, however, as she gradually began to escalate her questioning. Also, as time went on, she became more and more withdrawn. Her usual facial expression changed from one of contentment to one of worry. This really upset her parents. They started to feel increasingly guilty and wondered what they were doing wrong. On top of that, their sympathy and reassurance just didn't seem to be making things any better. They sought us out for some advice. Here's a step-by-step description of how Anita's behavior was changed by first changing the behavior of her parents.

1. DEFINING THE PROBLEM

After listening to Mr. and Mrs. R.'s description of the situation, we understood what the root of the problem was. They had been inadvertently rewarding Anita's insecure behavior with their attention. It all began way back when they responded so sympathetically to Anita's first "Do you love me?" statements. Thus, in behavioral terms, the solution to the problem lay in decreasing the frequency of those guilt-producing "Do you love me's."

2. MAKING EXPECTATIONS CLEAR

Anita's parents had tried without success to convince her rationally that she was loved. Most children's fears, however, just aren't that easily allayed by simple explanation. In fact, all that attention generally serves only to perpetuate the problem. We thus instructed Mr. and Mrs. R. to inform Anita that, although they loved her dearly, they were beginning to find her constant questioning somewhat annoying. As such, from now on they were simply going to ignore her whenever she engaged in that particular behavior. Anita protested, of course, but she understood exactly what her parents were saying.

3. IGNORING FEAR STATEMENTS

We practiced via role-playing the proper ignoring procedures with Anita's parents. We also emphasized to them the importance of being consistent with this technique. No attention whatsoever was to be given to Anita's fearful questioning, regardless of how persistent she became. Well, Mr. and Mrs. R. caught on quickly, and before long the frequency of Anita's questioning behavior began to taper off. The ignoring was working, but it still represented only one half of the total solution to the problem.

4. PRAISING ANITA FOR SUCCESSES

Ignoring taught Anita only what *not* to do. To help her learn what to do instead, we coached her parents in the fine points of effective praising. This was done simultaneously with the ignoring instruction. Once they had mastered the technique, we encouraged them to begin giving Anita lots of positive attention whenever she was engaged in more positive forms of behavior. When children resort to inappropriate means to obtain parental attention, that's often a clue that they simply haven't been getting enough recognition for behaving more acceptably. Thus, it's imperative that parents remember to praise their kids whenever they are pleased with what they're doing.

This explanation made great sense to Anita's parents, and they quickly began translating it into action at home. They started to spend more quality time with Anita, playing games, doing puzzles, conversing with her, and so on. The change in Anita was striking. No more repetitive questioning. No more worried looks. She had brightened up just knowing that the things she did were being noticed. She no longer had to ask if she were loved. She could tell just by the way her parents treated her. It was obvious now that they cared. By decreasing her fear statements via ignoring and encouraging more positive behavior through consistent praising, Mr. and Mrs. R. had started Anita back on the road to more self-confidence and trust.

Case #6: Mrs. F. and Her Shadow

Three-and-a-half-year-old Randy F. was tied to his mother's apron strings. He couldn't let her out of his sight for any more than several minutes at a time. As is so often the case with fearful behavior of this kind, Mrs. F. had originally been somewhat pleased by it. Randy was "Mom's little helper," and that was kind of nice. Once she realized that Randy wasn't interested at all in playing outside with the other kids, however, Mrs. F. became concerned. No amount of coaxing or encouragement would get him from her side for any great length of time. It only made him feel bad, which in turn made Mrs. F. feel worse. Mrs. F. was at a loss. She had no idea as to how she could change all this, so at a neighbor's suggestion she came to us. This is how we helped her.

1. DEFINING THE PROBLEM

The issue at hand was simply one of getting Randy to spend more time away from his mother. Evidently, being his mother's shadow had proven rewarding to him. To change his behavior, therefore, we had to find a way to make alternative activities even more rewarding to him.

2. PROCEEDING GRADUALLY IN SMALL STEPS

We knew that tossing Randy out of the house and locking the doors behind him would be too drastic. As we noted earlier in the chapter, sudden or intense measures usually serve only to panic, and perhaps even traumatize, a fearful youngster. Proceeding *gradually* in a logical and step-wise fashion thus became imperative. To accomplish this, we took advantage of Randy's desire to help and please his mother.

Step one consisted of Mrs. F. asking Randy to do something for her, such as dust or pick up toys, etc., in an *adjacent* room. At first, she assigned him tasks that would take him no more than five minutes or so to complete. Over the course of a week, however, she *gradually* lengthened these jobs to almost an hour's duration. Furthermore, she made it *clear* to Randy that he could help her best by staying in the other room until he'd finished his assigned chore.

The second step involved giving Randy things to do in rooms further away from the room Mrs. F. happened to be in. If she was upstairs, for example, she might ask him to straighten out the living room for her downstairs. Before long, Randy was able to spend over an hour out of his mother's view, as long as he was *in the house*. The next phase of the program, therefore, was directed toward getting Randy *out of the house* and playing with other kids.

This was accomplished in much the same way as Case #2 in this chapter—that is, Mrs. F. arranged for a neighbor boy of Randy's age to come over to the house each day. She told Randy that he could help her best by playing with the other boy, and she *gradually* increased the time requirement on this. To make it easier for the two boys to play together, she provided them with numerous games and other interesting activities to occupy their time. A week later, other neighborhood children were invited over. Soon Randy developed a wide circle of friends and, not surprisingly, seemed to care less and less about where his mother was or what she happened to be doing. One day, one of the kids suggested that they go over to his house and play on his new swing set. A minute later, they were all gone, Randy included. Since that day he has spent increasing amounts of his time out of the house playing with his friends. Randy didn't change completely overnight, but he's getting there. He's also a lot happier with himself these days.

3. PRAISING RANDY FOR SUCCESSES

Randy received lots of praise and attention at each stage of the program. His mother had role-played the praising technique with us, and she really made it pay off for her. Each time Randy showed even small progress, she gave him all sorts of positive attention. Once the other children started to come over each day, she supplemented her praise with candy treats and Kool Aid for all the kids. In this way, Mrs. F. helped create a warm and rewarding climate in which Randy could learn to feel more comfortable without her being present. It didn't take long for Randy to figure out that playing with his new buddies was a lot more exciting than being "Mom's little helper."

Summing Up

This chapter was designed to help parents help their children. First, we provided some general guidelines for you to keep in mind when dealing with your children's fears and insecurities. In addition, six case descriptions were included to show you how some of these techniques are used. Given this information, you should now be able to custom-tailor a home program to meet the particular needs of your child. By now, you ought to be pretty familiar with the basic principles of behavior change and relationship-building, as well as with a wide range of specific techniques. We trust that you'll be able to put them to work in your home. If you're not successful right away, however, don't give up. You may have to experiment a bit before hitting on a workable solution. The case examples we chose for this chapter were all shining successes. That's one of the reasons we presented them to you. Not all problem situations are resolved that easily, however. We occasionally have to revise our treatment strategies several times before finding a viable approach, yet we are constantly guided by the basic principles and procedures outlined in this book. It pays off for us, and we know that it can pay off for your family as well.

12

The Hyperactive Child

OF ALL the childhood disorders, hyperactivity is probably the best known. It is the single most common disorder seen by child psychiatrists in this country. Oddly enough, despite all that exposure, neither clinicians nor parents have a really clear picture of what hyperactivity is and what causes it. The goal of this chapter is to provide you with some information about this disorder, along with some gentle parenting techniques that make living with a hyperactive child easier.

The Cause of Hyperactivity

What causes hyperactivity? No one knows for sure. A few would argue that the way children are raised determines whether or not they will become hyperactive. This is essentially the *environmentalist* viewpoint, i.e., a child's environment ultimately determines what the child will be like. Most clinicians and researchers, however, feel that hyperactivity is a *constitutional* trait—that is, some children are born with a hyperactive temperament. Viewed in this light, certain styles of upbringing may make the problem better or worse, but at present, we know of no child-rearing techniques which can either prevent its occurrence or make it disappear entirely. Again, our aim in this chapter is simply to help you, the parent, make the most of an often frustrating situation.

Recognizing Hyperactivity

In addition to the debate about causes, hyperactivity research has also been plagued with a lack of true consensus around diagnostic signs. In other words, different people often have varying ideas as to the criteria used in labeling a child "hyperactive." There are, however, a number of behaviors or behavior patterns commonly associated with hyperactivity. They are:

1. Restlessness

When most people think of hyperactivity, they think of a child in perpetual motion. As a rule, the hyperactive child simply cannot sit still for very long. It's not that these kids move any faster than other children. If you were to see a bunch of school kids playing tag or rough-housing, for example, you'd be hard pressed to say which one was hyperactive. As soon as they entered the classroom, however, you'd probably spot the hyperactive child right away. He's the one who keeps going. He can't shut his engine off.

2. *Short Attention Span*

Hyperactive children are also noted for an inability to focus their attention on anything for very long. They tend to be highly distractible, and they usually jump from one activity to another. Of course, this often presents problems for them in school, both in terms of paying attention to their teachers and finishing class assignments. At play, a hyperactive child will often have all his toys out and scattered around, pausing for just a few moments to play with each one.

3. *Perseveration*

Paradoxically enough, some hyperactives will often get fixated in doing certain things and are seemingly unable to pull themselves away. If you ask a hyperactive child to hop *three* times on one foot, for example, he may well hop *five or six* times. We just finished telling you how hyperactives usually have a hard time sticking with anything, so it may seem somewhat contradictory to find out that they can also "get stuck" in certain activities. It's confusing, but that's the way it is.

4. *Lack of Affectionate Behavior*

In most cases, hyperactive kids are simply not "cuddlers." They're probably just too busy getting into other things. At any rate, whining, teasing, and bossiness are common characteristics of these children. They tend to be domineering in their relations with

206 | Special Situations and Specialized Procedures

other kids, and this often gets them into scrapes and arguments.

5. *Demanding of Attention*

Hyperactives seem to crave attention, from peers as well as parents. Ironically enough, when they get that attention, they're often still not satisfied. They seem insatiable in this regard. When you stop and consider for a moment the typical behavior repertoire of a hyperactive child, you can see that most of his actions are, in fact, terrific attention grabbers.

6. *Coordination Problems*

The coordination problems of hyperactive kids are of essentially two kinds. First of all, they tend to have poor control over *gross* body movements. This means that they are often less adept than other kids their age at playing ball, riding bikes, or any other activities which require balance, agility, or large muscle coordination. That's not all, however. Small muscle movements also tend to be poorly coordinated. Manual dexterity is usually not the forte of a hyperactive child. They typically print or write poorly, for example. Hand-eye coordination just isn't as well developed in these children as it is in other children their age.

7. *Forgetfulness*

Hyperactives tend to be forgetful. If you ask a hyperactive child to do something for you, he may well forget all about it within thirty seconds. This often angers parents, but these children aren't doing it on purpose. They simply have a hard time holding things in their memory.

8. *Impulsivity*

Hyperactive children get into things. What's more, they get into things *right away*. If they see something that interests them, they'll usually run right over to it and check it out. Hyperactive kids also find it difficult to delay gratification. If they want something, they want it *now*. And if you make them wait, they'll only make things a little more miserable for you. In this way, parents are often coerced into giving them what they want when they want it.

9. *Moodiness*

Fast swings in mood are another hallmark of the hyperactive child. One minute he can be happily playing with his toys—and just two seconds later he might be fighting with a sibling or whining to you for a cookie. In short, hyperactives tend to be temperamental, and that can be a trying thing for parents at times.

A Note of Caution to Parents

We have presented a list of behaviors commonly associated with hyperactivity. If you have read carefully, though, you probably noticed that some of those descriptions fit one or more of your kids. *That doesn't necessarily mean that they're hyperactive.* All children exhibit those behaviors at one time or another. Hyperactive children, however, do so with more *intensity*. In other words, they tend to be *excessively* restless, *excessively* demanding, and so on. This list can give you some clues about your child, especially if you have suspected hyperactivity for some time. Just remember, however, that this list of behaviors describes all children to some degree. It's best to be safe, and leave the task of diagnosis to a competent pediatrician.

The Role of the Pediatrician

In addition to diagnosis, the pediatrician is usually essential to the treatment of hyperactivity. The use of medication to treat hyperactivity has become increasingly widespread in recent years. The drugs most frequently used are the stimulant drugs d-amphetamine (Dexedrine) and methylphenidate (more commonly called Ritalin). These stimulant drugs are, paradoxically, usually effective in cases of hyperactivity. They are safe, provided their use is prescribed and regulated by a competent pediatrician.

What Can Parents Do?

We have told you what the pediatrician can do. He can prescribe medication for the hyperactive child, and in about two thirds of the cases, the children will respond well to these drugs. Medication, however, is not a magic wand. It's effective, but it's not the total answer. Hyperactive children benefit greatly from skilled parenting. Conversely, they can make life almost unbearable for unskilled parents. In this section, we will review for you some of the principles and procedures which contribute to successful parenting with the hyperactive child. Again, these skills aren't going to work any miracles for you. Your child will still be hyperactive. Nothing can change that. We can offer you, however, some ways to make both you and your child happier with each other. In other words, you'll both learn how to make the best of the situation.

Develop Your Entire Arsenal

If your child is hyperactive, you will need to be *maximally* effective as a parent. Of course, the best way we can think of for you to do that is simply by mastering *all* the material laid out in this book. Hyperactive children respond to good parenting techniques just like other kids. More than other parents, however, parents of hyperactives must be *quick* and *smooth* in their use of the primary parenting procedures. For this reason, we suggest extra practice on the role-playing scenes presented in Chapters Three through Six. Remember, when a child is hyperactive, things happen fast. It takes an alert and well-trained parent to stay on top of the situation.

We said earlier that hyperactive children demand a lot of attention. We also noted that their high frequency of inappropriate behavior usually coerces parents into giving them that attention. Of course, parental attention to misbehavior only serves to increase the probability that that behavior will occur again in the future. Thus, to change the behavior of a hyperactive child, or any child for that matter, parents need to systematically redirect their attention to more acceptable behavior. Effective parenting skills, i.e., praise, mild social disapproval, ignoring, and time out, are ideally suited to this purpose. They allow a parent to reward good behavior while simultaneously withdrawing excessive attention from the undesired behaviors. Again, even if you are proficient in these procedures, you probably won't turn your hyperactive child into a perfect angel, but you'll be a lot happier than parents who aren't proficient.

Important Points to Remember

We have stated that parents of hyperactive children must be maximally skilled in *all* phases of parenting. There are some procedures, however, which merit special attention and emphasis, and we will review those for you here.

1. Structure the Child with Clear Rules

Rules are very effective means of setting limits on the behavior of hyperactive children. It's a lot easier for parents to enforce preestablished rules than it is for them to "ad-lib" the rules as they go. In setting up the rules for your home, be sure that they are *simple, clear,* and *enforceable.* If you need some help in rule-setting, refer to the section of Chapter Four which outlines in detail the steps to effective rule-making.

2. Be Consistent

It's often difficult for parents of hyperactive kids to be consistent. It takes a lot of work, for example, just to keep track of what the child may be doing at any given moment. *Consistent* reward for constructive behavior, however, along with *consistent* punishment or ignoring of misbehavior, is essential to teaching your child what you expect of him. Consistency is especially important when it comes to enforcing rules. Some parents we know literally give up trying to cope with their hyperactive children. They allow their children to do essentially whatever they please. Sooner or later, however, one parent or the other will usually blow his stack. That is *not* consistent parenting. That only leads to more frustration on everybody's part and unnecessarily strained family relationships.

3. Immediate Praise for Appropriate Behavior

Children learn best when they are praised for doing something well. We encourage parents of hyperactives, therefore, to "catch" their kids being good and then praise them lavishly for it. One more thing: *Immediate* reward is especially important when dealing with hyperactive children. If you wait too long, they may be off doing something else and the effectiveness of your praise is thereby blunted. If you prefer that your child behaves in more positive ways, then you must reward him with your attention when he does.

4. Mild Social Disapproval

We have found that many parents of hyperactive kids tend to yell a lot. By the time we see them, most have come to accept yelling as a way of life, much as we have come to accept sunrises, wars, and air pollution. You can imagine, then, their astonishment when we tell them that they don't have to yell. They are even more surprised to learn that all of their yelling and attention aren't really punishments at all, but rewards instead.

Mild social disapproval works wonders. First of all, it's brief (less than three sentences), so you aren't really rewarding undesired behavior with too much of your attention. Secondly, it's low intensity, so you save wear and tear on your vocal chords and peace of mind. Finally, mild social disapproval is quick. It's ready to use, on-the-spot, in a wide variety of situations. Therefore, if you have a hyperactive child, you might do well to really master this versatile punishment technique.

5. *Time Out*

Time out is gentle, easy to use, and effective. It's a great technique for enforcing preestablished rules. Perhaps the major advantage of time out, however, is that it gives everyone a chance to "cool off." If your hyperactive child has been getting way out of hand, for example, time out will provide a much needed break in the action.

6. *The Role of Special Incentive Programs*

As a rule, we don't recommend that parents rely on tangible rewards. Special incentive programs are *not* a substitute for good parenting. If your child is very young, however, you may have to supplement your parenting skills with such a program. If so, make sure that you don't let the tangible reward program carry the entire load. You still need to use social rewards and punishments effectively. After all, no parent really wants to see his child on a special incentive program forever. Heavy emphasis on social rewards and punishments, therefore, is needed to make it easier for you to eventually phase out the tangible reward program.

Specific Areas Where Parents Can Help

We have reviewed some basic considerations for parents of hyperactive kids to keep in mind. Basically, each contributes to making you a highly competent parent, equipped to deal quickly, effectively, and lovingly with a wide variety of situations. There are also a few other, more specific things that parents can do to help their hyperactive children grow and develop more normally. Attentional difficulties and coordination problems are two areas in which parents can aid their children. Let's look at the problem of attentional deficits first.

Attentional Deficits

The hyperactive child is notorious for his short attention span. As we mentioned earlier, this can cause the child some problems in school. You can help, though, if you're willing to put in a little time working with your child at home.

Basically, your approach should be much the same as the strategies outlined in Chapter Ten, describing the slow learner. That is, choose *easy* and *interesting* tasks, such as puzzles, coloring, etc., for the child to do, *gradually* increasing the time required to complete those tasks. Be sure to reward him for task *completion*, not just correctness. Thus, instead of saying, "Boy, did you do a good job," you might say, "Boy, I think it's wonderful that you finished the whole thing."

Three other considerations are important here. First of all, avoid criticism. Instead, help your child have a good time. Second, choose a work area free of distractions. Hyperactives find it difficult enough to concentrate on one thing for very long, without having to contend with frequent interruptions, noise, and so on. Finally, give the youngster a rest break now and then. You can even use these breaks as rewards for finishing the task at hand. At any rate, allow the child a chance to move around occasionally. It will help him work off some of that excess energy, thus making it easier for him to do a better job on the home attention exercises.

Large Muscle Coordination

If your child has difficulty coordinating his larger muscles, you can help him simply by getting him to practice these movements. Have him practice jumping, walking on tiptoe, or any other activities which develop balance and agility. If possible, try to make it more fun for him by inserting these activities into a game format. Athletics and dancing are also fine developers of gross body coordination in children.

Regardless of the specific nature of the activity, however, keep the following considerations in mind. First of all, make the tasks easy and interesting. You have to sustain the child's enthusiasm. Second, continually praise the child for *sticking with* the exercise, and praise him *while* he's doing it. Finally, make the experience a pleasant one. Avoid criticism for failure and provide frequent rest breaks along the way.

Fine Muscle Coordination

In the beginning of this chapter, we pointed out that hyperactive children often have difficulty with tasks requiring small muscle coordination. As such, any exercises which require manual dexterity and hand-eye coordination are bound to be helpful. Drawing, playing with tinkertoys, printing, and writing are good examples of these kinds of tasks. Again, proceed *gradually* with your child, always making sure that you reward him for *finishing* the exercise. Avoid pushing him to do too much at one sitting. In that way, he'll be less likely to give up.

A Pause to Review

We have discussed a number of specific things that you can do at home to further your child's development. You probably noticed that the procedures had a lot of elements in common. Let us review those elements here again, this time in list form.

1. Keep tasks and exercises fairly easy
2. Proceed gradually
3. Reward immediately
4. Reward task *completion*
5. Keep tasks and exercises interesting and varied
6. Avoid criticism
7. Provide frequent rest breaks
8. Don't try to force the child to do something he really doesn't want to do.

If you adhere to these general guidelines, the chances that your hyperactive child will benefit from home training will be substantially increased.

The Punishment Trap

For the most part, parents of hyperactive kids come to us looking pretty ragged. They're tired, frustrated, and sometimes rather depressed. One of their major complaints is that they are sick and tired of constantly having to punish their child. They have fallen into what psychologists commonly refer to as the "punishment trap."

The punishment trap is essentially an attitude, a negative attitude. After months, or perhaps even years, of frustrating attempts at child discipline, many of these parents become pessimistic. They tune in only to what their child is doing wrong. Criticizing, yelling, and spanking typically become a way of life in these families. Of course, this is understandable, but it's also very unfortunate. This kind of attitude usually stands in the way of constructive behavior change and more harmonious family interactions.

Before anything else, therefore, we explain to these parents the importance of adopting a more positive outlook. After all, hyperactivity is not the child's fault. In most cases, a hyperactive child does not really go out of his way to irritate and annoy his parents. It just seems that way, that's all. Hyperactives do, however, respond to *firm, loving,* and *consistent* parenting. They respond, as other children do, to praise and attention for constructive behavior. For that reason, there is cause for optimism. To climb all the way out of the punishment trap, however, requires that parents do a complete turnabout in the way they view their children. Instead of noticing only misbehavior, they need to "catch" the child being good. Then, by rewarding good behavior immediately and lavishly, they can effectively encourage their children to behave in more desirable ways. Think for a moment about how you relate to your hyperactive child. Do you have a negative attitude that's causing you to notice only what he does wrong? Or are you alert to the good things he does as well? Remember, appropriate behavior must first be *noticed* before it can be rewarded.

Hyperactivity and Self-Concept

It's not unusual for a hyperactive child to develop a negative self-concept. He tends to be scolded and criticized a lot, and after a while, he begins to believe what his parents, teachers, and even other kids are saying about him. Let us show you what we mean. Here's an excerpt from a recorded interview with Mr. and Mrs. B. and their hyperactive son, Ronald.

Mrs. B.: Let me tell you, he gets into everything. If I leave him alone for even a minute, God knows what he'll do. He picks on his sister, pesters the dog, breaks things—you name it and he does it. (Deep sigh.) Quite frankly, we're getting a little fed up with all this.

Mr. B.: And don't forget to tell them what Ronny's teacher said.

Mrs. B.: Oh yeah, it seems that Ronny's been a real headache for her, too. She said she's going to fail him if he keeps going the way he has. He's at the bottom of his class, and, worse yet, he doesn't seem to care at all.

Mr. B.: We know he can't help it, but is there anything you can do to help?

Us: Well, what do you think of all this, Ronny?

> Ronny: (Squirming:) I don't know. I'm not a very
> good boy, I guess. Hey, can I look at those
> magazines over there?
>
> Mrs. B.: No! Sit still.

Mr. and Mrs. B. were obviously concerned, but their frustration was even more obvious. The most noticeable thing about this particular interview, however, was the way Mr. and Mrs. B. talked about Ronny *right in front of him.* When parents do this, it's not surprising that their children start to think of themselves as "bad boys" or "dummies," etc. And even though it's true that they "can't help it," hyperactives don't need to hear that all the time. It only makes them feel unusual or inadequate, and that, of course, doesn't help them one little bit.

So, if possible, try to avoid excessive criticism of your child. It's all right to punish when it's deserved, but derogatory comments usually only make matters worse. If you get into the habit of calling a child "impossible" or "lazy," for example, he'll quickly begin to see himself that way. And once that happens, he will be even more likely to act that way. Again, try to focus on the positive aspects of your child's behavior, and if you need to punish, be specific. For example, saying, "Ronny, I don't like it when you pester the dog. Stop it!" is far more effective than saying, "Oh Ronny, you're getting to be a real pain in the neck." The first statement is about *behavior.* It tells Ronny what he was doing wrong, and thus, he can learn from it. The second statement, however, is a derogatory comment about Ronny's personality. From this he learns only what someone thinks of him, i.e., that he's a "pain in the neck." He learns nothing about what he should or shouldn't do. At any rate, just keep in mind that your child usually believes what you tell him, as well as what you tell others about him. If you keep your statements specific to *behaviors*, you probably won't run the risk of developing a negative self-concept in your child.

Summing Up

Hyperactivity is a common childhood disorder. Research data indicate that the symptoms of hyperactivity usually decline as the child matures, often disappearing by age twelve. It is best to deal with hyperactivity as soon as it is recognized, however, in order to prevent later, more serious consequences such as poor self-concept, repeated school failure, and social inadequacy. At any rate, if you suspect that your child may be hyperactive, have him checked out by a pediatrician. If the child is indeed hyperactive, the pediatrician may also prescribe some beneficial medication for him.

Parents of hyperactive kids need to be maximally effective in order to cope with their children. A positive attitude and the consistent application of solid parenting techniques are major steps toward making families happier.

13 ⤳⧢⧢⤳

When to Consult a Professional

THE PRINCIPLES and procedures outlined in this book are gentle, effective, and easy to learn. In short, they'll get you through almost any child-related situations you may encounter as a parent. In this book, we've given you the essentials. It's up to you, though, to take it from here. You now have the opportunity to master these skills through role-play practice in the privacy of your own home. We hope you'll take full advantage of that opportunity.

Lest you be lulled into believing that this book has *all* the answers, however, let us assure you that this is not the case. There are times when it may be appropriate, and even necessary, for you to consult a professional about your child's behavior. In this last chapter, therefore, we will briefly outline for you a list of those kinds of situations which are best handled with professional assistance.

When Nothing Works

We assume that you've learned and practiced the procedures presented in this book. If you have, and things still haven't improved, you'd better seek professional advice. You might be doing something wrong, or maybe the problem is more severe than you had originally thought. In any case, a competent professional should be able to help you straighten out the situation.

Learning Problems

In Chapter Ten, we noted the importance of obtaining professional advice and assistance for the slow learner. Psychological testing is usually essential to diagnose the specific cause of the problem. Only when you know specifically what you're dealing with can appropriate remedial measures be taken. A professional person trained in the area of learning-related problems can be invaluable to you, both in terms of determining a suitable school placement and/or in coaching you in ways to work effectively with the child at home.

Hyperactivity

Both from a diagnostic and a treatment standpoint, hyperactivity requires professional help. Medication has become the treatment of choice, and, of course, this can only be prescribed by a physician.

Bizarre Behavior

This area is less clear cut. It's often hard for parents to decide what's normal and what isn't. If you have some doubts about your child's behavior, however, it's probably best to have it checked out.

Normal kids will often do things which may appear "crazy" to adults. Anyone who has observed a youngster conversing with an imaginary playmate can vouch for that. Yet, for many kids, imaginary playmates are no more than a part of growing up. As a rule of thumb, however, if your child begins to behave in ways that strike you as weird, strange, or bizarre, that may be a tip-off that something is seriously wrong with him. Head-banging, repetitive movements, severe and prolonged depression, unusual sexual behavior, or delayed onset of speech are just a few of the behaviors which may indicate a deeper underlying disturbance. Again, when in doubt, check it out. It never hurts to be on the safe side, especially when the well-being of your child is concerned.

Antisocial Behavior

By antisocial behavior, we don't mean shyness or poor manners. What we're talking about here includes a variety of *high-intensity* behaviors performed at the expense of others or their property. Fire-setting, theft, and extreme cruelty are common examples of antisocial behavior. The repeated use of "hard" drugs and/or alcohol also falls into this category. Antisocial behavior is extreme, as well as dangerous. If you notice that your child is beginning to behave in this fashion, get some professional help right away. The longer you wait, the greater the chances are that someone will get hurt. And if that happens, you and your child may well find yourselves up to your ears in legal problems.

A Word about Responsibility

Consulting a professional does not mean that you can simply turn your problems over to someone else. That's just not the way it works. What it really means is that now, perhaps more than ever, you need to be a skilled and concerned parent. Raising your children is a responsibility you don't want to avoid. You can make it a positive experience for you and your family. We hope that you have found this book helpful in that endeavor.

INDEX